THE PAST & THE CURIOUS

For more history, humor, and interesting people from the past, check out Mick Sullivan's award-winning podcast *The Past and The Curious*. The monthly audio production is a favorite of families around the globe and has been featured in *The New York Times*, *Mental Floss*, *The Times of London*, and *School Library Journal*.

The show is available for free on all podcast platforms or at **www.ThePastAndTheCurious.com**

THE PAST THE CURIOUS PRESENTS

I SEE LINCOLN'S UNDERPANTS

THE SURPRISING TIMES UNDERWEAR (AND THE PEOPLE WEARING THEM) MADE HISTORY

By Mick Sullivan

Illustrated by Suki Anderson

Heart Ally Books, LLC
Camano Island, WA

Published by:
Heart Ally Books, LLC
26910 92nd Ave NW C5-406, Stanwood, WA 98292
Published on Camano Island, WA, USA
www.heartallybooks.com

ISBN-13: 978-1-63107-047-1 (paperback)

ISBN-13: 978-1-63107-048-8 (epub)

ISBN-13: 978-1-63107-049-5 (audiobook)

1 2 3 4 5 6 7 8 9 10

For my Mom, who indulged my curiosities, made sure I always stayed young at heart, and bought all of my underwear for much of my life.

And for Owen and Ben. Don't stop laughing. Also, do you have clean underwear on right now? (That goes for everyone, really.)

CONTENTS

PREFACE
(Why I wrote a book about underwear)

Sometimes when I'm reading a book about the past, a random sentence will stop me in my tracks. Once, I came across a detail about a nineteenth-century ferry boat that was powered by horses walking on a treadmill. It blew my mind and I had to lie down for days. A similar feeling happened when I was reading a book about the Brooklyn Bridge. Out of nowhere, the author included bridge engineer Washington Roebling's true recollection of seeing Abraham Lincoln's underwear make an embarrassing appearance. I was in an airport when I read that, so I couldn't really lie down, but the entirety of the flight was spent imagining Abe's feelings on the matter (and also imagining his underwear — I'm not gonna lie).

As I read more and more about people, it became apparent that even the most famous, the most heralded, and most impactful people were just that: people. And if there's one thing that equalizes us all, one thing that ties us all together, and one thing that will always get a laugh, it's underwear. We all wear it. Garrett Morgan was no different. Queen Victoria, Buster Keaton, and Abraham Lincoln weren't, either. As you'll see in these stories, sometimes their underwear made history of its own.

Every person in this book made a big mark on history. And each one of them was a real person with strengths, weaknesses, flaws, and unique abilities (yes, and underwear). We all are.

I hope this book will introduce you to new people worth knowing, show you a new side of people you already knew, and inspire you to learn more about stories that aren't often told in history books. You never know what you'll find.

I also hope you'll have fun; I sure had a blast writing it.

I See Lincoln's Underpants
Abraham Lincoln (1809–1865)

When he was young, Abraham Lincoln's family was packed into their tiny one-room cabin like smelly sardines in a tiny tin can. If everyone else had walked out the door and left the little guy alone, it still would have been a tight space for baby Abe. Luckily, cramped quarters were not something he'd need to deal with as an adult. His last home, the White House, was definitely roomy enough for him to stretch out his full-grown six-foot, four-inch frame.

Today he towers above the rest as the tallest president America has ever looked up to, but no matter where he hung his stovepipe hat or how fancy his oversized outerwear might have been, his underwear never really changed much. From the backwoods of Kentucky to the halls of Washington, DC, his simple, homemade drawers were as honest and plain as the man who wore them. At least that's what the evidence we have seems to indicate. The few surprise appearances of his plain white whites would have left plenty of other people red-cheeked and embarrassed. We've all had those kinds of nightmares. Lincoln's legendary sense of humor most certainly helped him handle these very real — and very revealing — moments.

When Abe first opened his eyes in that little cabin, he was in Hodgenville, Kentucky. He lived there with his  mom, dad, and sister until they packed up and moved to Indiana. After his mom died, his father married a woman with a few other kids. Abe liked her very much, which was fortunate because he couldn't really say the same thing about his father.

His old man was as rough as their underwear. Thankfully, laundry day brought sweet relief. The kids would hand over their uncomfy, homemade undies for washing and a few hours of freedom. Their new cabin was a little larger, but there wasn't really much to do other than wait around in his birthday suit until the wash was dry. Ever the bookworm, Abe passed those bare-bottomed hours reading the classics.

Reading was typical for him. If anyone ever went looking for Abe, they'd usually find him with his nose in a book. On the contrary, his father preferred him to have his butt in the field, getting sweaty from working the land. Luckily for the rest of us, his stepmother saw how important an education could be to the boy and supported his desire to learn. That's probably why he liked her so much. Rather than cutting wheat or splitting rails, he really preferred to sit in the shade, reading and writing. At the age of 21 he bid his family adieu, packed up his books, filled a bag with some clothes and a few pairs of underwear, and set out to see what the world had in store for him.

Don't think Abe was lazy. In his new home state of Illinois, Abe did a lot of hard work. He was a soldier. He dug canals. He piloted a flatboat. He was a shopkeeper, a bartender, a lawyer, a politician, and even a wrestler.

When he was the new guy in the town of New Salem, the lanky and lean Lincoln was the target of curiosity for many townsfolk. For some local bullies known as the Clary's Grove Boys, he was the target of scorn — or more accurately, their misplaced insecurities. These bullies weren't ready to confront their feelings like mature adults, so they confronted Lincoln with their anger instead.

Even if the bullies were acting like punks, Lincoln knew he couldn't back down from a challenge if he hoped to earn the respect of the rugged folks in the far-off town. So he accepted the challenge of a wrestling match with one of the bullies. People of New Salem found out what Abraham Lincoln was made of that day. Though accounts differ on who won, the Clary's Grove Boys were eager to vote for Lincoln in any election with his name on the ballot from that point on.

With each new addition to his resume, Lincoln discovered that many people liked him. He could be honest and kind, was stronger than most, loved a good laugh, and seemed to always have a story to tell. Abe was usually the smartest man in a room, and his goals were as high as the stars that were always just out of the reach of his long arms.

Abe's first role in politics was a seat in the Illinois State House of Representatives. Years later he served a term in Congress in Washington, DC, as a representative from Illinois. His intelligence and ability were well known, but he really got people's attention in 1858 when he ran as the Republican candidate from Illinois for US Senate against a man named Stephen Douglas.

Abe and his opponent travelled across the state of Illinois, attracting large crowds for their thought-provoking political debates. Let's face it: packing into a sweaty room or standing in the sun on a cobblestone town square to watch two guys without microphones talk for three hours was probably nowhere near as interesting as a wrestling match would have been. Those days were behind Abe at this point, though. Plus, there's very little evidence that Douglas was much of a wrestler, anyway. It probably wouldn't have been a fair fight.

Despite the lack of physical competition at the debates, Abe still boasted some overly enthusiastic fans. One night in Ottawa, Illinois, his cheering squad hoisted the giant man onto their shoulders to celebrate a particularly good debate performance. Maybe these rabid fans had nothing else more exciting to cheer for. It's more likely that they were genuinely moved and excited by what their candidate had to say. Either way, they made Abe their champion.

As he was bobbing around on shoulders, soaking in the chants and celebration, the legs of his pants started to rise. It was August, a time most people would have left their long underwear at home, but Abe was not like most people in this regard. A little (or actually a lot) of sweaty wool never bothered him. Within full view of his fans, the watchful eyes of his adversaries, and the constant scrutiny of the press, Abe gave

them more than anyone bargained for. Out popped Abe's long underwear.

The showing made the news and garnered plenty of knicker-related snickers. Abe lost that election. Of course, he didn't lose to Douglas because of the underwear, but it certainly didn't help. Though Douglas won the Senate seat, it was Lincoln who came out on top in the end. His star was rising, and the debates helped to make him a household name. When the presidential election came around in 1860, he would be the Republican nominee. The field was crowded and several other nominees split the vote, and in the end Abe was the last man standing.

Not long after he put his undies in a dresser drawer in the White House, the American Civil War began. Unhappy with Lincoln's stance against slavery and what they believed to be a threat to their rights as a state, South Carolina seceded: they left the Union. Then they opened fire on an offshore fort filled with Americans still loyal to the president.

From there, things got uglier. South Carolina was followed by other slave-holding states who were concerned with preserving their economies and way of life, which were built on the enslavement of other human beings. Lincoln long ago had said that he did not expect America to split, but that he believed it would be all one thing, or all the other. It was his mission to hold America together, and eventually, in doing so, end slavery in every state.

Men rushed to enlist on both sides. The Yankees of the North wore blue, and the Confederates of the South wore gray. Keeping those guys clothed in their blues and grays was a difficult task. The North had more factories to churn out clothing, but the war dragged on for years, with hundreds of thousands of men marching every day. They usually found their wardrobe to be lacking, to say the least, and there was no easy way to get replacement clothing to the soldiers on the war front.

After the Union lost the Battle of Bull Run in 1861, Lincoln paid a visit to the field to see the men. One officer from Wisconsin was upset that his men were under-supplied. He tried to explain that better clothing and equipment were essential and would help give Lincoln the victories the North needed. To prove his point, he grabbed one of his soldiers and turned him around.

The man's rear end was all the evidence the president needed. Peeking from the split seam of his Union-blue pants was a white flag of truce — a funny name the soldiers gave their underwear. Lincoln, quite used to wearing homemade undies of his own, probably saw no real problem with the soldier's skivvies. The all-too-common split in his pants, though? That was definitely a dressing dilemma. The officer's point was as easy to see as his soldier's underwear.

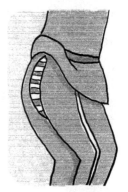

Throughout the war, Lincoln was no stranger to many of the other the soldiers in the field. Before or after battles, during training, and even in the hospitals, Abe would make the rounds. It was important for him to understand what the men were going through. It was also important for the men to see him and know that they had his support. In general, a visit from the president was something the men looked forward to, but one unlucky regiment of soldiers saw a bit more of him — and his support — than anyone had really hoped.

Just before the Battle of the Wilderness in 1864, Abe approached a group of soldiers on horseback for another day of reviewing the troops. Though he was a great lawyer and a pretty good wrestler, he was never much of a horseman, which the men immediately noticed. He fumbled around uncomfortably on the back of his horse. Once safely dismounted from his not-so-trusty steed, a series of unfortunate events unfolded, which brought the focus of every private on parade to the poor president's pants.

"Soon after the march began his stovepipe hat fell off; next his pantaloons, which were not fastened on the bottom, slipped up to his knees, showing his white, homemade drawers, secured below with some strings of white tape, which presently unraveled and slipped up also, revealing a long, hairy leg. While we were inclined to smile, we were at the same time very much chagrined to see our poor President compelled to endure such unmerited and humiliating torture."

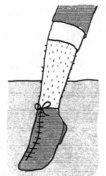

According to Washington Roebling, who wrote this observation, Lincoln quickly got over the embarrassment of showing his underwear to the crowd and continued with the review. Like anyone else, Abe put his drawers on one leg at a time, but the men were probably surprised to clearly see that the president's underpants were as plain and simple as their own.

Less than a year after his underwear-exposing wardrobe malfunction, Lincoln would lead the Union to victory and reunite the country. Of course, he'd give his life in the end. Less than a week after the Confederacy surrendered, Lincoln was assassinated while watching a play in Washington, DC. He was buried in 1865, wearing the same suit he proudly donned at his second inauguration ceremony.

That historic outfit saw the light of day one more time, 36 years later in 1901. Surrounded by dozens of nosy onlookers, his body was exhumed before being moved to its current resting place. Curiosity got the most of the crowd, and it was decided to open the casket one last time before he was permanently covered in concrete. According to witnesses, the beard that still covered his chin was as black as the day he was buried. His suit, however, was grimy and had mildewed over the years. The grubby clothes kept anyone from seeing what his underwear looked like, but it's safe to say they were probably grimy and mildewed, too. That might not have been far off from how they would have been when he was walking around in them.

George Washington's Outhouse… or Conference Room?

If you ever visit Mount Vernon, George Washington's home, you won't see any of his underwear on the tour. But that doesn't mean other people didn't see his most intimate apparel in person. Before the days of plumbing, people used outhouses when nature called, and Mount Vernon is home to one of the most unusual outhouses you'll ever see. There are not one, not two, but three potty holes inside the spacious structure. As far as historians can tell, it is likely that these would have been used at the same time, with little concern for privacy. Was it an honor — or impossible — to do your business alongside George Washington? Luckily, we'll never know.

SHORT SHORT

HARRY S. TRUMAN, PRIVATE PRESIDENT

Before Harry S. Truman became the 33rd president of the United States, he owned a haberdashery, which is a store that sells men's clothing and accessories. In addition to suits, ties, and hats, shoppers could pick up a pair of silk underpants from the future president.

Harry's mother taught him many things, including the belief that a man should wash his own socks and underwear. When he became president in 1945, his staff was surprised that he refused to throw his socks and undies in a pile for someone else to clean. It was common to see him scrubbing the soiled items in a sink just off of the Oval Office. His mother must have been very proud.

No Privacy for the Queen

Marie Antoinette (1755–1793)

Once upon a time, royal families lived ridiculously public lives. Any given palace was filled with overly privileged courtiers who were ready to kiss any royal heinie they could. To make matters worse, many of these courtiers had "Rights of Entry," which meant they could watch the king or queen do nearly anything. These privileges could include watching a monarch get into their underwear, bathe (not that bathing was very common), or even give birth. Why this was desirable is not easy to understand today, but let's just agree that life (not to mention privacy) was very different back then.

Maria Theresa, the empress of the Austro-Hungarian Empire, decided she was having none of that invasive nonsense. She was a brilliantly powerful woman who eventually gave birth to 16 children, all of whom she regarded as giant diaper-wearing game pieces for her lifelong game of international royal-family chess. In her plan, each chess piece — er, child — would be married off to other royal courts when they reached the maturity of their teenage years. Her meticulously arranged marriages would extend the influence and power of her royal Habsburg Family.

Most of her kids were born to a room full of witnesses, but by the time her penultimate (fancy way to say "second-to-last") child was born, she was done with birthing in front of a live studio audience. She finally decided those nosy neighbors would have to wait outside. This daughter, named Marie Antoinette, was born in relative peace and quiet, but it was pretty much the last time she'd ever enjoy privacy from the eyes of royal court-iers. In fact, it would get much worse for Marie.

No one really expected much out of Marie Antoi-nette. To be fair, it's hard to get much attention when you're the 15th child. She wasn't really challenged with an education and she didn't really seem excited about one, either. Music excited her, though, and her skills on the piano were well respected. It is said she won the heart of a prodigy named Mozart when they were both youngsters. By all accounts she enjoyed her childhood.

Those carefree days in Vienna ended when her father died while traveling. Not long after, the disease small-pox proved that it could devastate a royal family just as easily as it could punish a family of peasants. When her brother's wife died from the viral infection, Maria Theresa took Marie Antoinette's older sister, Josepha, down to the tomb to pay respects. There's a tale that the tomb wasn't completely sealed, and that Josepha ended up getting smallpox from her sister-in-law's dead body. If it's true, that's certainly a terrible (and gross) last gift. Perhaps she wound up with the disease through less haunting ways, but in any case the results were the same. The disease soon  claimed the life of Marie's newly-infected older sister Josepha, which threw Maria Theresa's plans out of whack.

There had already been a wedding scheduled when the tragedy struck and Josepha was supposed to be marrying a young prince in Spain. Understandably, this young man's family had little interest in having him marry a dead girl. Since it was a royal-family chess-move marriage, the poor guy didn't really have a say in it either way, but it's fair to assume he wasn't interested in a corpse bride, either.

So all of Maria Theresa's daughters moved up a notch. The upset order of arranged marriages changed everyone's plans, and after every girl was assigned a new husband-to-be  in the matrimonial lottery, Marie Antoinette learned she'd be marrying an awkward young man in France who would someday be the king of the powerful nation. He was then known as Louis Auguste, but someday he'd be Louis XVI.

When it came time to leave her palace in Vienna and head to her new home and husband in France, there were so many carriages, people, and horses in the procession that it was like an entire city was traveling across the countryside. As the future queen of France, the fanciest carriage of all was hers, of course. Every little thing inside was trimmed in velvet and gold – including her commode and bidet. A crowd of people watched her use these on a daily basis.

Being used to peering eyes during these private moments soon came in handy. When they arrived at the French border, the caravan of carriages was met by an equally large French fleet for the official handoff of the bride. Like a queenly baton in a royal relay race, the 14-year-old girl would pass from country to country, only crossing the finish line at the magnificent palace of Versailles. Unlike a race, though, no one was really in a hurry. Literally everything in these days required an elaborate ceremony, and this would be no different.

On an island in the Rhine River, she slowly stepped away from the hundreds of people who had brought her, and towards the hundreds of people who awaited her. Then she took off her clothes. All of them. It's like that dream we've all had where you go to school in your underwear, except instead of school, it was royal court. And instead of a dream, it was very real. The ceremony was meant to symbolize the end of her Austrian life. She would be purely French now. From  that moment forth, she'd wear no Austrian makeup, no Austrian clothes, no Austrian jewelry, and no Austrian underwear. Her undies, and everything else, would be French forevermore.

Hundreds of eyes watched as someone brought her French-made replacements and waited patiently as she put it all on. There was a chemise, which is a white linen dress undergarment, followed by a corset, which tightened around her torso like a big boa constrictor. Inside the fabric of the corset were ribs of whalebone, and when the laces were cinched, the contraption squeezed all the air out of her, squishing her organs like sausage in a casing. It didn't get any better with the giant forms beneath her skirt and panniers; these were giant cages that tied to her hips and protruded off to each side.

The saying "Beauty is pain" might actually be an incomplete saying. The full thing could more accurately be, "Beauty is pain…and also never being able to get comfortable…and also never being able to easily fit through a doorway."

After squeezing through a door in her French finery a few days later, she finally came face to face with her future her husband. Sparks did not fly. Marie didn't find the 15-year-old boy particularly attractive and felt he was pretty awkward in general. He wasn't terribly excited, either. In his journal, the only thing he wrote about the fateful day was "Met the dauphine today." Not a real charmer. To be fair, he was still practically a child like Marie, so the idea of having to get married probably scared him out of his wits!

On the morning of their wedding, Marie stood shivering in the cold, drafty room that had belonged to her husband-to-be's dead mother (before she died, of course. She wasn't still there. They buried her. Don't be gross). As the dauphine, Marie had to show patience and kindness on her face, but her head was probably swimming with cuss words she wanted hurl at the group of attending ladies, known as her ladies-in-waiting. "Why were they called the ladies-in-waiting?" she probably wondered. Marie Antoinette was the one doing all the waiting around.

It took hours to get ready. They slowly piled her hair high upon her head and powdered it like a big furry doughnut. Her face was slathered in makeup and then the ladies rouged her cheeks. After what seemed like hours, they brought out her underwear. First, a shift that was tied with lace around her body, and then the rest of her large and bulging under-structure. Finally came the dress, which was inflated by everything underneath like a balloon from the Thanksgiving Day Parade.

Since her mother-in-law was no longer living, Marie would be the most important woman in the French court. One day soon the relative stranger to France would be queen. So every single eyeball was watching her closely. Her wedding dress had to be incredible. It was. There was just one small problem, though. The dressmaker made it before Marie had arrived from Austria. She had never actually sat for a fitting, and as a result it was a tad too small. Despite her slender build and a team of women pull-

ing in all directions, the back of the dress could not be completely closed. This left a bit of her underwear peeking out. There were many catty courtiers in attendance who were eager to watch her embarrass herself. Poor Marie's exposed underwear couldn't have made them any happier.

Years later, when Louis's grandfather died, the inevitable happened. Louis never wanted to be king, and he hoped his father and two older brothers would wear the crown instead. But they, like many other family members in this story, croaked before they could. Marie was okay with it. As the queen, she was a celebrity living a life of luxury, splendor, and fine fashion, but also unpleasant odors. The palace at Versailles had 1100 rooms, and the never-ending maze of halls and walls often made it hard to find a restroom. As a result, many of the otherwise fancy rooms smelled like port-a-potties in the hot summer sun. It was pretty common for people to relieve themselves wherever they could get a little privacy, something Marie might have even envied. Because of this (and plenty of other reasons) she spent most of her time in her own separate, private house on the land.

Still, she hated waiting for the ladies-in-waiting to finish arguing about who got to wash her feet and who got to tie her corset. In fact, she got sick of wearing corsets altogether. When she paraded with friends around the gardens in her shift, which was basically a plain cotton underdress, people started talking. When she wore the same thing to an official court function, the talking grew louder. This wasn't just a rejection of customs; it was undignified, in the eyes of many. All those fancy noble heads underneath fancy hats practically exploded over the queen basically wearing her underwear in public.

To be clear, it was just a plain, white, billowy dress, but to the people in her world, it was underwear — something worn between her perfume-laden body and her fine French fabric dress. Marie didn't care. To prove that point, she had a portrait painted of herself wearing the cotton shift, so now anyone and everyone could see it. Despite the uproar her underdress painting caused, the attention it garnered helped inspire other women to dress more simply. She was a trendsetter, after all, and maybe, deep down, other ladies hated wearing an entire closet's worth of fabric every day, too.

So the feedback wasn't all bad. Thanks to Marie, women's fashion in France got simpler and easier for a period of time. This wasn't really what the citizens of France were worried about, though. While Marie was complaining about waiting for her ladies to tend to her daily routine, and while the royal courtiers were just complaining about Marie, citizens of France were complaining about real problems. They didn't have any food or money. Several harsh winters left the peasants with no crops; they didn't even have the basics to bake bread. Understandably, they got really angry when they thought about Marie, Louis, and the rest of their courtiers living in extravagance. So began the French Revolution.

When the revolting peasants first stormed the palace, the angry mob just ransacked the joint. While they were smashing up whatever they could get their hands on, the royal family made a quick, quiet escape. It wouldn't be so easy the next time. People leading the French Revolution wanted to end the rule of kings and give power to the citizens. Inspired by the American Revolution, which Marie's husband, King Louis XVI, had ironically helped pay for, the French citizens wouldn't rest until they had a democracy.

Part of not resting meant cutting off a bunch of heads with the newfangled head-chopper-offer known as the guillotine. King Louis was at the top of their to-do list. While Marie was locked in a dark jail cell, she might have heard the cheering crowds when her husband's head fell into a basket. It would be months before Marie would know her own fate, but the writing was on the wall. One last time she felt the sun on her face and the wind in her hair. She was carted to the gallows in her cotton underdress. It was much like the one she wore in that scandalous painting from happier days.

Royal heads come off just as easily as anyone else's. Marie's was no different. The rebels threw her top and bottom into an unmarked grave near her two-piece husband. It was an undignified final resting place for both of them.

Years later, after the president-turned-emperor Napoleon met his own end, the French monarchy returned and Louis's younger brother was crowned king. The new king was irked by the indignity his brother and sister-in-law were suffering in the afterlife. With the royal family back in power, there was no reason for them to moulder amongst mere peasants and other less important headless nobles. He ordered that they be dug up and reburied in a more fitting tomb. It is rumored that the strong-stomached gravediggers were able to identify Marie Antoinette's headless and decayed body amongst the other rotten corpses — by the very specific stitching of her underwear.

PANNIERS

(pronounced pan-YAY)

History has seen all sorts of ludicrously large types of apparel for ladies to wear. But an undergarment that required new furniture to be created just so ladies could sit down? That's a special kind of underwear. Carrying the weight of gobs and gobs of fabric stretched over internal structures surely got exhausting. It is unfair that a normal couch didn't even have the space for a lady to relax for a minute. Hopefully she had some friends to catch her when she fainted.

The name *panniers* comes from the French word for the wicker baskets that were slung over the back of pack mules and donkeys. This makes sense when you look at a dress with panniers. At the hips, the fancy fabric juts out a great distance, making the woman's form extremely wide from the waist down. It's not bell-shaped, though.

The protrusions on the side leave the outfit relatively flat at the front and back. This shape is created by two giant structures, almost like birdcages, which are tied around a lady's hips on each side. These were usually made from whalebone and varied in sizes from "hide a puppy inside" to "hide a group of preschoolers inside."[1]

Historians argue about a lot of things, and one of those things is where panniers made their miserable debut. Some say it was the ladies of Spain who first filled up space at parties with the aid of the undergarment. Others say it was in England. Regardless of where you land in this terse debate, we can agree that most people think of France when they think of this giant form of fashion. It was here in the courts of Paris and Versailles that women most famously squeezed down hallways one at a time, rested their rumps on doublewide seats, and undoubtedly knocked over anything within a close radius that wasn't nailed down.

Fashions at this time had a different sense of balance than they do today. Many of these monstrous panniers were wider than the woman was tall, which might have served her own physical balance well enough but made everything else a chore. Many panniers measured up to seven feet in width!

---

[1] I'm not saying people actually did sneak around five or six kids in their panniers, but let's just say they could have if they needed to.

CAUGHT WITH HIS PANTS DOWN

Charles Lee (1732–1782):
George Washington's Frenemy

Historians have been pretty silent on the subject of George Washington's underwear. Maybe they feel funny airing the first president's dirty laundry, but, in reality, George had plenty to be embarrassed about. Like us all, he was far from perfect. One poor decision he made as a young soldier basically started the French and Indian War. So if you ever feel bad about a mistake, just remember that your questionable actions will probably never spark international conflict.

It'd be nice to believe that, whether he was starting wars or ending them, George Washington still stepped into his underwear one leg at a time. It's not that straightforward, though. On a visit to his house, you might wonder, *where is all the underwear?* Historians from Mt. Vernon (George Washington's home, which is now a museum) believe that George didn't wear underwear at all. Instead, he likely wore a long shirt, which he wrapped and tucked underneath — sort of like a diaper. Try not to laugh when you think about that the next time you look at his face on a dollar bill.

One man who was okay with letting George's dirty laundry flap like a flag in the breeze was his fellow general, Charles Lee. As far as we know, Lee never brought up George's diaper shirts,[2] but he made sure to point out every other embarrassing matter, personal shortcoming, and monstrous mistake in George's life.

Charles Lee was probably jealous of George because he believed that *he* should've been the one in charge of the American army instead. If you know anything about American history, you know his wish never came true.

Most people have never even heard of Charles Lee, which is a fact that would probably drive him crazy to know. Unlike their robust reverence for George today, Americans certainly don't celebrate Lee's birthday with mattress sales and a day off school. And they definitely haven't built gigantic stone obelisks in his honor, in a

---

[2] Probably because he was wearing one, too.

town that also bears his name. It's probably for the better — Lee, DC, isn't a very catchy name for a capital city. It's not as if he didn't try to carve his place in history, though. Charles Lee's story can serve as an interesting reminder that things could've worked out very differently. What if it had been Charles in charge?

Charles made it well known to Continental Congress decision makers like John Adams and Benjamin Franklin that he wanted Washington's job and all the glory that went with it. He believed he deserved it with every fiber of his being, and he wasn't completely alone in that belief.

It was pretty easy to see that he was the most qualified candidate for the job. Charles Lee had one big problem, though: no one really liked him. It can be a big red flag when you can't get along with anyone and are a poor teammate. As a result of his unwillingness to play well with others, Charles would eventually set the table for his own downfall, and find his own underwear shining in the bright light of day, to boot. Meanwhile, George would go down in history with the mythic record and pristine, private underpants Charles Lee wanted for himself.

Charles Lee was born the very same month of the very same year as George Washington: February of 1732. Lee opened his eyes and cried his first of many cries in England, an ocean away from infant George. Lee's father was so desperate to have a soldier for a son that

he enlisted Charles in the army at the ripe old age of 11. This may have had something to do with Charles's general unfriendliness.

For the rest of his life he was busy doing army stuff. He was a career soldier with a chip on his shoulder. One of his favorite things to do was criticize his superiors in letters whenever they made mistakes (which, as we've already seen, anyone can do). It was common for him to call his boss "stupid, ridiculous, and absurd" or a "blockhead" who is "sunk in to idiotism." And all that was just about one guy. Luckily for Charles, that blockheaded boss never saw the insulting letter. Luckily for us, a historian did!

The French and Indian War would bring him to America for the first time in 1754 as a lieutenant. Another 21-year-old soldier fighting for the British, named George Washington, basically started the war when he launched an ill-advised attack on French troops in present-day Pennsylvania. Despite the severe misstep, Washington's subsequent deeds helped him become internationally known by the end of the war, which was unusual for a British soldier who never set foot in England. Most of the army, including Charles, looked down their noses at the British subjects in America. And Charles had a very long, skinny nose to look down.

By the time Charles left the American continent he had risen to the rank of captain, married the daughter of a Mohawk Indian chief, had two kids, suffered a pretty nasty injury, and insulted all of his commanding officers. He didn't think they were fit to polish his boots, much less lead soldiers in battle.

It was probably for this poor attitude and his quick temper that his Mohawk in-laws called him "Boiling Water." It was also fitting because boiling water turns to steam and disappears, which is precisely what he did to his Mohawk family when it was time to go back home to England. In fact, no one knows what their names were because he never even mentioned them in any of his letters or writing.

Landing alone back in England, he found no wars to fight, so he picked fights of his own with anyone who disagreed with him or didn't live up to his ridiculous expectations. Eventually the British army grew sick of him and decided to pay him half of his annual wages if he'd just retire.

He accepted the deal but was still craving glory, so he became a soldier of fortune. This meant other countries

hired him to fight in battles across the European continent. In exchange for money, he led troops and gleefully
stuck swords and lead balls into people. It was a pretty
gruesome way to earn a living — but at this time, military glory meant a lot to a guy like Charles. Plus he was
getting great battle-leading experience and building up
his resume.

At this same time in America, George Washington
resigned from the army, hung up his uniform, and was
raising his family, while dabbling in local politics and
overseeing Mt. Vernon, his estate, which depended on
the labor of enslaved people.

In 1773, three years before the Declaration of Independence, Charles Lee returned to America. Clearly
not a Father of the Year candidate, he made no effort to
find his wife and kids. However, he was sure to surround
himself with a bunch of dogs. Outside of war, dogs were
the love of his life. This was probably by necessity, since
very few people could actually
stand to be around him. Plus, with
a canine crew, he'd be leader of at
least one pack. It was common to
see him traveling with five or six of
his favorite pups.

Though he was still technically a soldier in the British army, Charles decided to join the American patriots

in their disagreement with Great Britain and the growing disdain for King George III. The disdain part came naturally to him.

Charles could easily get behind the idea of hating authority, but he may have genuinely felt like America deserved independence. On the other hand, he may have just been excited to know that if there was a war, he was in an opportune position. After all, he wholeheartedly believed that he was the only logical choice to lead an American army. That was just the glorious kind of role he could really sink his teeth into.

He was right: no one else on the continent had more battle experience, but with a guy like this, it's hard to be certain of his motives.

Either way, when the war broke out after America told King George to take a hike, the job of leading the army was given to Washington. Charles Lee wasn't completely left out in the cold. He was given a good position leading troops as a general, but he wasn't top dog.

This made Charles very angry and he spent a lot of energy trying to make George look bad. But while George and the other revolutionary rabble-rousers stood in opposition to the King of England, they did so distinctly as Americans. Sure, Washington had been an officer in the British military, but the bad taste it left in his mouth led to his resignation way back in 1759. He was a traitor to the crown, but not *the worst kind* of a traitor. The same thing could not be said for Charles. First, Lee was born in England, which was a big difference in the eyes of his countrymen. Also, since he was still officially a British officer, his revolutionary behavior was especially revolting to his former teammates. Outside of winning the war outright, there was nothing British soldiers wanted more than to catch him.

But life at the top wasn't easy for George Washington. In the winter of 1776, things looked bad for the American cause. Washington had not won a major battle (though Lee had some success, which he told everyone about constantly), and the city of New York fell into British hands. It looked bad for the American patriots. The redcoats chased the embarrassed and overmatched, rag-tag American army out of the Big Apple and into the future Garden State of New Jersey. Washington travelled at the head of one large group of retreating soldiers, while Lee was leading another, larger group many miles away. Washington wanted them to rendezvous — meet up and travel together — so he sent carriers on horseback to deliver letter after letter to Lee. Lee did not react. It was a poor decision to ignore the orders, but then Charles Lee committed an unforgivable act. He decided to spend the night away from his troops at White's Inn in the little town of Basking Ridge, New Jersey.

To a degree, it's understandable. It was December and he was probably tired of the icy cold that froze the East Coast, but he knew better than to leave his troops. With just a few of his officers and guards, he enjoyed a meal, stoked a fire, and took off his uniform to relax. Wearing his dirty dressing gown, which was about all he had for underwear, he tucked himself in for a cozy night of sleep in a nice, warm bed. It was certainly better than the cold, hard ground his men would have that night.

When the next morning came, groggy Charles was slow to rise. Wiping the sleep from his eyes, he found his way to the table to write some letters, still in his dirty dressing gown. Maybe he was finally going to respond and tell George he was on his way. Or maybe he was complaining to someone else about what a dunce he thought Washington was. Either way, his concentration was broken by the thunder of horse hooves coming down the lane.

Not all Americans were in favor of independence from Great Britain. The people who remained loyal to the King of England were known as Loyalists. One such Loyalist had noticed Charles Lee and his small party of men the day before. Wishing to demonstrate his unflappable loyalty to the crown, this man told some British soldiers where the unfriendly American general was staying. The idea of capturing the traitorous and unlikeable Lee had the British soldiers practically salivating like one of Lee's dogs pouncing on a hambone.

When they stopped in front of the inn and called out, Lee's surprised men scattered like ants in every direction. Lee was not much braver. One report said the frightened and underdressed man panicked and tried to hide in the fireplace. It was pointless, though. He was trapped in his morning dressing gown.

Banastre Tarleton, the man in charge, made it easy: Charles Lee could come out with his hands up, or they would burn the place to the ground. This 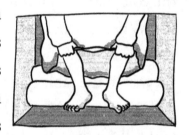 was an upsetting thing to hear for the poor woman who owned the place, but even more so for Charles. It was the end of the line, and he knew it. There would be no need to light a fire. To the delight of the British soldiers, when Charles Lee stepped out into the morning sun he was still wearing his underwear.

It's hard to imagine a more undignified surrender of an officer, which probably made his enemies savor it even more. Lee was not even given the courtesy of his uniform coat. They strapped him to a horse just as they had found him, threw a blanket over top, and rode all the way to New York City.

Despite not liking him, the British, much like Charles himself, believed he was the best soldier in America. They figured with him imprisoned, the war would end soon. This would not be farther from the truth. Just a few weeks later, George Washington would lead the soldiers in the famously underwear-freezing Crossing of the Delaware to the Battle of Trenton. This reinvigorated the American cause and finally gave people the belief that an army led by George might have a chance after all. Still, the war would not end for seven more years, in 1783.

As it turned out, Lee was doubly traitorous. While he was imprisoned, Charles Lee drew up plans for the British on how to beat the Americans. Luckily for him they would not be discovered until long after his death.

PAUL REVERE, LEGENDARY UNDERWEAR SNEAK

Paul Revere's dramatic horse ride to warn American patriots that the British soldiers were invading Boston is one of the most famous moments of the American Revolution. Before he began the horseback portion of his evening, Revere had to sneak across the Charles River in a rowboat. He would encounter many challenges that night, but his first was a pair of noisy oars. Fearing the squeaky paddles would be heard by the British soldiers and give away his position, Paul and his small party of patriots needed a solution.

He and a friend ran to a nearby home and called up to the second story window. When they roused the sleeping woman inside, they loudly whispered the details of their precarious paddle predicament. As an American patriot herself, she was willing to help, and soon one of her petticoats came floating down from the window. The undergarment gift from above was a satisfactory solution. The men used the petticoat to muffle the oars against the side of the boat, allowing Revere to cross quietly and alert the Americans that the British were coming!

Molly Pitcher, Carried off By Cannonball

There probably wasn't a real Molly Pitcher. It is believed that the legendary name is more of a composite character representing many different American women who helped on the battlefields of the Revolutionary War. The idea of Molly Pitcher could have been inspired by any number of brave women.

One likely candidate is a Pennsylvania woman named Mary Ludwig. She travelled with the American army along with her husband, who worked a cannon for the artillery team. Mary would often tend to the wounded and carry water to cool the cannons before they were refilled with explosive black powder. Colorful firsthand accounts from the Battle of Monmouth tell of how she joined her husband in operating one of the cannons when his fellow soldiers could not.

As she worked to reload the weapon, an enemy cannonball came barreling towards her. By sheer luck, the hefty projectile passed perfectly between her legs, taking part of her petticoat as it passed. Mary barely reacted. According to one witness, she simply remarked that if it had been a bit higher, it would have carried away something else more important instead. Luckily her torso remained attached, and she kept on fighting.

UNDERDRESSED RESCUE
Garrett Morgan (1877–1963)

While growing up near Paris, Kentucky, Garrett Morgan's dresser wasn't filled with the soft, white drawers he'd heroically show the world later in life. Just as his underwear and pajama selection left a lot to be desired, the early circumstances of his life didn't offer a plethora of options, either. Days brought hard work — probably while wearing scratchy burlap undies, which were the common, quick, homemade-underwear solution of the day. Nights might have brought much needed sleep, but it was still in those same uncomfortable undies. A home full of older and younger siblings meant most of those undies had been, or were bound to be, someone else's undies. This is the way it was with pretty much everything else in the house, too.

For the first part of their lives, Garrett's parents had been enslaved. When the American Civil War brought an end to slavery in the United States, Mr. and Mrs. Morgan remained near the plantation where they had once lived. When baby Garrett came along in 1877, they were working as sharecroppers and raising a constantly growing family. Sharecropping is mostly what it sounds like, though people were typically pretty loose with the whole "sharing" part. Landowners allowed tenant farmers to grow crops on land in exchange for a large share of the profits. In most cases, the landowners helped themselves to the largest share — though the tenants did the labor. Between the hard work of farming, teaching, and feeding eleven growing kids who probably ate more than their fair share of the sharecropped crops, Garrett's parents had plenty to worry about. They may have wanted to give their kids an education, but it wasn't something they could easily afford.

In general, public schools were a thing of the future for Garrett's time and place. Though some larger cities might have had full public education available, it was not the norm. It wouldn't even be until Garrett was 41 years old, in 1918, that American children were legally required to finish elementary school at all. His occasional schooling, which he crammed in between working on the farm, amounted to a sixth-grade education. Had there been more free public school to show up to after sixth grade, walking through the door wouldn't have been a problem — he was always looking for new ways to feed his brain.

Early on, Garrett figured out that using the brain in his head was his superpower. The boy had a knack for figuring out how things worked and solving problems when they didn't.

At 14, he packed a few shirts, a pair of pants, and some undies that he wouldn't have to share, and went north to Cincinnati, Ohio. Alone in the city, the barely teenaged boy soon found work as a handyman. Earnings were spent on two things: staying alive and learning. After paying for food, a room, and the occasional new article of clothing (he was still a growing young man, after all), he used the rest of the money to hire private tutors. Obviously, Garrett was responsible in addition to being smart. These teachers-for-hire helped him stitch together the pieces of a formal education to complement the real-world experience he was wrapping himself in already.

A few years later, he made the fateful decision to move farther north to Cleveland, Ohio. He had heard that the largest clothing factory in the world was here, in addition to dozens of other shops filled with thousands of people who cut, stitched, and sewed everything wearable under the sun and moon. Each day, a never-ending parade of baby dresses, men's suits, women's skirts, and an assortment of underwear were finished, packed, and shipped out to cover rear ends all across the country.

Built on the banks of Lake Erie, Cleveland was a major center in America's garment industry, so it was a good place to be for a smart kid with a mechanical mind. Of course, no one knew what brilliance was swimming around between the ears of this new arrival, so Garrett started at the bottom: sweeping floors. He quickly found a way to stand out. While he swept up the fabric scraps and threads he noticed a problem. The constant use of the sewing machines around him loosened the belts which drove the engines. This slowed down the people working, since the machines required regular maintenance and repair. Not only was he able to repair the machines, but he devised a solution that kept the belt tight all day. Before long, he was an official shop mechanic.

In 1901 he sold that first invention, a sewing machine belt tightener. Garrett was a man who liked to solve problems, so it was the first of many. Soon after, he was playing around with some chemicals in search of a way to lubricate thread so it wouldn't burn when pulled quickly through a machine.

When he casually wiped the new goop from his hand on a rag with curly fibers, Garrett was amazed to see little ringlets and tangles completely straightened. Wanting to confirm what he observed about the potion, he asked to borrow a neighbor's curly-haired dog. When the animal returned home, the owner didn't recognize the little pup. Garrett's creation had magically straightened the hair and temporarily left it look-  ing like another dog entirely. With some more tweaking, Garrett realized his concoction would make a great hair straightener for people, too. Eventually he sold the hair tonic under the company name of G.A. Morgan Hair Refining Company, but for the time being he kept working in the clothing shops, slowly moving towards his destiny.

When he took a job with a new employer, he met a young German woman named Mary Hasek. She was a seamstress, and before long they were practically stitched together at the side. Unfortunately, prejudice found them. The shop's owner told them he wouldn't employ a black man who was in a romantic relationship with a white woman. Garrett was told to end it or find work some- where else.

Garrett quit on the spot. As usual, he had better ideas, anyway. Soon, they'd sew together their love, energy, and collective batch of skills to open a new business together. They found their feet with a sewing machine repair shop to serve the many facto-  ries in Cleveland but soon hit their stride when they later opened the Morgan Skirt Shop.

Garrett could do nearly anything with a sewing machine. The fancy zigzag stitches and custom machine refinements he created made some of the most desirable and durable skirts, pants, and undergarments people could ever wish to cover themselves with. As sales took off, their staff of workers grew by the dozens. Long gone were the lean days of his youth — Garrett and Mary built a life filled with meaning, success, children, and even a few inventions on the side. While his first inventions were for convenience and productivity, his next one would save lives.

One major problem that plagued clothing factories at the turn of the century was fire. A 1911 blaze at New York City's Triangle Shirtwaist Company made national news when it claimed the lives of 146 factory workers, mostly young women. While this was one of the largest factory fires in history, it wasn't the only one. Eventually, industrial disasters like this would lead to strict safety regulations for workers, better emergency escapes, and even the exit signs you still see in public buildings today.

Garrett knew firsthand how devastating fires could be. Back home in Kentucky he had seen neighbors lose everything when shacks burned down. In 1909, grown-up Garrett would watch another neighbor's place go up in flames. Only this time it was a Cleveland clothing factory, like the very ones he had spent many years inside. Along with everyone else on the street, he stood watching help-lessly. He wasn't alone in realizing that there was no way for a would-be-rescuer to safely enter a smoke-filled building, but he was alone in deciding that he would do something about it.

When he put the finishing touches on his Safety Hood and stuck his head inside for the first time, he might have scared the pants off of his family. The world was a long way from the outlandish costumes of Star Wars or any other science-fiction fantasy movies in 1914, but Garrett's new getup would be a perfect onscreen fit for even the most eccentric modern space-movie franchise. The large canvas mask covered his entire head and came

to a sharp point at the top. He could peer through small windows near his eyes. To prevent smoke from getting inside, the hood fit tightly around his shoulders. Finally, from the area around the chin, two gigantic, elephant-trunk-like tubes protruded and hung almost to the ground. While it might appear nightmarish to some, Garrett had dreamt up a new gas mask — one which would prove to be, by far, the most effective to date.

There's nothing more convincing than a little thrilling drama to show people why they need a new invention, and Garrett knew this. Outside of firehouses across the country, Garrett set up a big tent which was filled with smoke from wood, tar, chemicals, and even animal manure. Then, confused firefighters watched him dress up like a superfan 90 years too early for a Star Wars cosplay convention. Once in costume, Spaceman Morgan would disappear into the tent tendered with twigs and tar and teeming with terrible poop-smoke. Onlookers expected to be rescuing the man in the mask from suffocation within seconds, but when he strolled out smiling 20 minutes later, the firemen instead opened their wallets.

Many rescue workers and fire departments wanted Safety Hoods for themselves, and Garrett was happy to oblige. They didn't put out the welcome mat everywhere, though. When he visited some places in the American

South, he found people unwilling to buy an invention, no matter how great, from a Black man. This made Garrett angry, but he resolved to sell his device despite the ignorance and hate. To fool the willfully foolish even further, he simply hired a white man to pretend to be the inventor. Masked Garrett still did the ol' stinky, smoky tent trick to prove the invention worked — and still cashed the checks for the sales of the lifesaving solution.

Despite the ignorance and injustice he saw in the world, Garrett was committed to his own success. One key was a good night's sleep. Most evenings he'd slip into his long, white, underwear-like pajamas and tuck himself into bed feeling pretty good about things. The little boy from Kentucky had businesses, a great new invention, a beautiful family, and he even had a phone — one of the first in Cleveland. So it might be ironic that this very phone woke him up in the middle of the night on July 24, 1916.

The frantic voice on the other end of the line told him there was a terrible disaster at the Water Works tunnel being dug under Lake Erie. The tunnel collapsed with workers trapped inside, and when that happened, there was a release of poisonous gas into the tunnel's airway. It was hard to know how many people were still alive inside, but it was certain there were some. First responders ventured into the pressurized tunnel to help but were overcome by the noxious fumes and had to be rescued themselves. No one was sure what could be done, but one of the men on the scene had recalled seeing Garrett's mask in action. This man figured if the Safety Hood could keep someone safe in a tent full of ammonia and manure smoke, then maybe it could help someone find the tunnel's survivors despite the fetid fumes. Garrett agreed. There was no time to waste.

There wasn't even time to put on clothes. Those long, white drawers he had donned before departing for dreamland would have to do. Indecency doesn't matter in a life-or-death ordeal. Arriving quickly enough to make Batman jealous, two brave men appeared at the tunnel entrance with gas masks in tow. It was Garrett and his brother. Neither was wearing proper clothes. Undeterred and without a hint of embarrassment, the pair threw the cumbersome canvas cowls over their heads and ran into the stinky darkness of the tunnel.

The fresh air on the outside was of little consolation for the people who paced and prayed there for what seemed like hours. When they finally spied a figure that looked like an alien in underwear, carrying a full grown man as if he were a sleeping baby, the crowd was again able to breathe as easily as Garrett. The Safety Hood was a success. Everyone who survived the gaseous explosion, yet remained trapped inside, was soon rescued by the Morgan brothers.

In the months that followed, many Americans would find themselves overseas on the battle lines of World War I. A sinister new technology debuted during this conflict. Weaponized gases were used to suffocate and harm large groups of people at one time. Garrett's Safety Hood was a big step towards a new gas-mask that was used to keep people safe in the face of the chemical warfare that was raging around them.

With each invention and business victory, Garrett was able to focus more on the things that mattered most to him. In 1919, he founded Cleveland Call, one of the most important newspapers for Black communities in America, and in 1923 he patented his most famous invention — the three-position traffic signal. This revolutionary invention led to our modern-day red, yellow, and green lights — and it also led to another financial windfall for Garrett. General Electric, the company founded by Thomas Edison, paid him a staggering $40,000 for the rights.

Despite the near-constant successes and occasional heroic rescues, Garrett still witnessed and experienced racism. Barred from joining a country club in the area, he used part of his profits to purchase land and founded Ohio's first country club for Black citizens. When villainous members of the Ku Klux Klan tried to intimidate Garrett and his friends by burning a cross on the land, he and his brothers fought back and chased them off. Whatever Garrett said or did must have worked, because it's reported that the terrorists never came back.

When Garrett passed away in 1963, he left a legacy of creativity and drive, not to mention the financial security his gifts brought to his surviving family. He'd be the first to tell you he didn't get the honor he deserved in his lifetime. Many are surprised to learn that he was

never compensated nor acknowledged by national hero commissions of the day for his daring tunnel rescue. Despite that, he firmly knew who he was and how he mattered in his America. His modest tombstone in Cleveland reads, "By his deeds he shall be remembered."

TIGHTEY-WHITIES

When you wore a hole in your pants back in 1935, or decided to finally replace those dirty underclothes peeking through, you might head to a department store to update your wardrobe. One of the biggest of these department stores was Marshall Field's in Chicago. They had everything you could imagine, and even some things you couldn't. Fashion changed fast in the 1930s, but Marshall Field's always had the latest and greatest. Just after Christmas the store received a shipment of a brand-new kind of underwear. You might call them briefs, or Y-fronts, or even tightey-whities today, but they were first known as "jockeys."

Jockeys were introduced by a company named Cooper's, whose original focus was selling socks to lumberjacks. It was good business, but they were always on the lookout for something they could sell to everyone else. The chance came when one of their designers got a postcard from a friend in France. Pictured in the beach scene was an unfamiliar kind of men's bathing suit. These small swimsuit pants would soon inspire their next big product.

On January 19, 1935, the faux-French undies debuted in a spot front and center on the shelves of Marshall Field's. Once everything was in place, the manager glanced at the day's weather report and saw that Chicago was expecting a blizzard. Filled with doubt, he wondered if people would want to buy something so skimpy and small when the weather was so bitterly cold. Something like long johns made more sense, he reasoned. So he told the employees to pull them back off the shelves and display some of the warmest, itchiest long johns they could find.

Before they could even get started, the staff looked around and realized that they had nearly sold out of the unfamiliar new underwear. By noon that day they had sold 600 packs of the underpants without even trying. Customers were eager to own the short, Y-front unmentionables. The briefs were such a winner that Field's stores reportedly sold 30,000 in the first month.

Tightey-whitey popularity soared, and Cooper's couldn't make them fast enough at first. Employees were eventually able to meet the demand of the new under-wear-hungry public...and then some. With boxes upon boxes of brand-new briefs, the company promoted the surplus skivvies by chartering a special jet plane to deliver the undies around the country. The airmailed underwear eventually landed in the top drawers of most homes. Perhaps as a result of the sky-high promotion, comfort, low price, or just their good design, the once-fresh fad has covered rear ends for generations of people now. There are probably some in your home (or covering your rear) right now.

Up, Up, and Away Went Their Clothes

Jean-Pierre Blanchard (1753–1809) and
John Jeffries (1744–1819)

A duck, a rooster, and a sheep in the basket of a hot-air balloon might sound like the setup for a joke, but this jet-setting petting zoo was a very real thing. In 1783, floating farm animals to the clouds was how the Montgolfier brothers convinced King Louis XVI of France that their new invention was safe. The king was a bit worried for the safety of any people in the airborne vehicle, so he requested a few test flights with something less human. No animals were harmed in the making of this story, so Louis gave the ballooning brothers his blessing. This set the stage for France to lead Europe in flight for decades.

Truthfully, it's a wonder that the flying flock wasn't hurt. We wouldn't call the Montgolfiers' balloon *safe* by the standards of today. It was essentially made of wallpaper, which is a poor match for the open flame it needed to rise. One errant ember could have turned the beautiful balloon to a flaming fireball. Unfazed by the possibility of pyrotechnical problems, the brothers soon took the place of the animals in the basket themselves. It was the first of many flights they'd make, and amazingly they avoided hitting the ground all of their lives.

Someone who *would* eventually hit the ground was another Frenchman named Jean-Pierre Blanchard. Long before Blanchard came crashing to the earth, he was testing the limits of flight in a unique balloon of his own. While the Montgolfier brothers were flying their hot-air balloon, Blanchard chose the newly discovered gas hydrogen to lift his own. Hydrogen is the lightest element on the periodic table, which makes it lighter than air.

Jean-Pierre realized that if the gas were captured in a sack (like a balloon), it would float. Get a big enough sack, tie a basket to it, hop in, and, before you can say "dirigible," you're on your way to the clouds. One note: before it was commonly known as hydrogen, it was called inflammable air. Contrary to your instincts, *inflammable* means the same thing as *flammable*. This is also bad news for flames — just ask the captain of the Hindenburg blimp, who would learn this in 1937.

Jean-Pierre Blanchard didn't use any flames, though; he had a crazier idea. Once he got his big balloon off the ground, he thought he would be able to glide through the air like a boat on a lake. On this hunch, he made a hand-cranked propeller and big silk air paddles — kind of like wings on sticks.  If the story of human creativity has taught us anything, it is that some ideas work and some do not. Those air paddles most certainly did not work, but anything is worth a shot. On the bright side, his balloon sure did float.

It floated so well that a man named John Jeffries became a financier. Being an aeronautic pioneer is expensive. The cost of materials and upkeep on a balloon, buying hydrogen, traveling to launch sites, and everything else all added up very quickly. Jeffries was tremendously excited and interested by the possibilities of flight, so he helped Blanchard pay for all of this. But, like the basket hanging from the bottom of Blanchard's big balloon, there were strings attached.

Jeffries was an American doctor who had remained loyal to the King of England during the American Revolution. The revolting Americans didn't take too kindly to loyalists at the time, so Jeffries left for Europe. He carried a curious passion for understanding how weather worked and saw the balloon as a way to learn more. As he figured it, his money should earn him a seat on the balloon with Jean-Pierre.

It wasn't just a seat on any flight that he had his heart set on. Jean-Pierre was planning to make history by crossing the English Channel, and John wanted to be along for *that* ride. The flight would be the very first overseas international balloon flight.

Each man knew it would be a historic achievement, but neither could really do it without the other. So Jean-Pierre Blanchard begrudgingly agreed. They'd fly from England to France over the narrow arm of the Atlantic Ocean that separates the two countries. If successful, they'd go down in history. If unsuccessful, they'd go down in the English Channel, winding up with wet undies (best case), or as fish food (worst case).

The distance between Dover, England, and Calais, France, is only about 20 miles, but it was still a wildly dangerous thing to attempt. The men would find themselves at the mercy of the wind. This meant it would take hours to travel. They'd also have to be very careful about what they brought with them, because the balloon could only lift so much weight. It was no big deal to sink from the sky somewhere over the countryside, but a dirigible descending somewhere over the salty deep was another matter entirely.

If we could go back in time and check Jean-Pierre's report card from school, it would probably say, "Jean-Pierre is very smart and gifted, but he does not play well with others." While Jean-Pierre agreed to let Jeffries join the flight, it was probably just to appease the American. In reality, Jean-Pierre had no intention of sharing a  single ounce of the foreign-flight fame and glory. The finicky Frenchman tried nearly every dirty trick he could think of to keep John Jeffries sulking on the ground and not by his side in the basket.

At the launch site in Dover, the overly dramatic Jean-Pierre suddenly ran to his room screaming (probably something about never learning to share). In an immature display, he then locked himself inside and refused to come out. His hope was that John would give up and just go home. The exiled American wasn't going to give up easily, though. Jean-Pierre Blanchard lost that battle of wills and soon the men found themselves together in the basket of the balloon. But Jean-Pierre still wasn't ready to share the airspace.

When the balloon was finally untethered from Earth, the big moment was disappointing. The hydrogen-filled sack above their heads was no match for the full basket at their feet. Apparently heavy with cargo, tools, and the men themselves, the balloon couldn't leave the earth. The overweight basket surprised John. He had double-checked all of the calculations and was certain that it should've lifted the load. But there was no denying it now: the basket was too heavy.

At least that's the way the conniving Jean-Pierre wanted it to seem. He put on an Oscar-winning performance. Dripping with feigned sorrow and fake remorse, he informed John that as much as he *hated* it, it would appear that the balloon could only carry one man. Since he was the only *actual* balloon pilot, and since it was such a dangerous endeavor, the safest option would be for John to just let him go on ahead on his own.

John was not going to fall for it. His sharp eye caught a glimpse of an unfamiliar leather belt peeking out of the break in Jean-Pierre's jacket and he demanded to know what was under his clothes. At this demand, Jean-Pierre stammered and protested but knew it was no use. He pulled back his jacket to show a fanny-pack, which he had filled with lead. This was the real reason the balloon was not lifting off! The persistently pesky aeronaut had no other tricks up his sleeves. He knew he'd have to toss the lead and share the basket. Putting their disagreements behind them, they joined their fates, finally setting sail in the skies.

As the balloon lifted, the men were surrounded in the basket by the ineffective silk air paddles, biscuits, brandy, a host of scientific equipment, and a bag full of letters bound for French citizens. Expecting to make history and wanting to look good doing it, the two men were dressed in some of their finest clothes.

As they left the Cliffs of Dover behind and below, everything seemed to be going well enough. The idea of becoming fish food was the farthest thing from either man's mind, but things soon changed. Somewhere over the waves of the channel, long before the coast of France had come into sight, both men agreed that they were slowly getting closer to the water below. Of all directions to be moving, down was the worst.

The descent was not dramatic at first, so there was no real need to panic. Obviously they had brought a lot with them, and if they needed to lighten the weight in the basket, there were certainly a few things they could do without. On such a relatively short journey they could live without the brandy and bread. Perhaps tossing those few pounds would get the balloon moving back upward, they reasoned. The goods splashed into the ocean and the men made observations to see if this did the trick.

It did not help. A tiny twinge of panic, like a single bubble in a glass of soda, raced up their bodies. They looked over to see the salty water a little bit closer than it had been before. Without hesitation, the silken air paddles and propeller were also tossed into the froth. When the pair peered over the side again, the water was even closer still. Several more bubbles of panic raced up their bodies.

The telescope, compass, and assortment of scientific tools had been expensive, but they wouldn't be of any use to a scientist who was sleeping in Davy Jones's locker. With a nervous gulp and a Hail Mary prayer, these, too, were tossed out of the basket. The valuable instruments sank to the bottom of the English Channel.

Still, the balloon slowly sank closer to the water. After tossing the bag of mail, there was nothing left to jettison. The terrified twosome were all that remained in the basket of the balloon. Meanwhile, that same basket was perilously close to being swallowed by the sea. Those fizzy bubbles of panic in their bodies were now overflowing like a bottle of soda hurled across a room. Neither was willing to give in to a watery fate, but they had reached the end of their plan. Obviously, too much weight was the problem, but with nothing left to toss, they were stuck. Then it clicked: *Pee*. Every little bit of weight mattered in a situation like this and the men pinned their remaining hopes on a few ounces of urine.

Unfortunately the weight in their bladders was not enough to save their lives. With literally nothing left — no telescopes, no bread, no packages, and no pee — the men gulped one last gulp, felt the mist of the water that was now frightfully close, and took off their clothes. Fancy shoes, velvet jackets, linen shirts, and expensive trousers joined all of the other lost loot in the lapping waves. Two scared men in their underwear were all that remained.

It certainly seemed like the end was near for John Jeffries and Jean-Pierre Blanchard. The only relief came from the fact that no one would be around to watch them die in their underwear.

Then a miracle happened. Like a gift from the heavens or a goddess satisfied with the offerings and sacrifices they had tossed into the sea, a merciful breeze began to blow. The men filled their lungs with the first breath of hope since the ordeal began, and the wind lifted the balloon steadily above the threatening waves. Unbelievably, the coastline of France soon came into view. Growing relief washed over them as the dry land continued

to creep closer and closer. They were finally brought to a stop by a tree near the French coast, where they dangled until help arrived.

The joy and gratitude of surviving such a harrowing ordeal far outweighed the embarrassment they felt when a crowd of confused French citizens from a nearby town came to investigate the strange purple globe. As surprising as that might have been, perhaps more so were the two empty-handed, undressed men dangling in the basket.

They actually hadn't thrown everything out. There was one piece of mail addressed to Benjamin Franklin, who had happened to be in Paris at the time. Wanting to get it to the important American, Jeffries decided to hide that letter in his underwear, rather than throw it over with the rest of the mail they had to purge. Once the pair were fished out 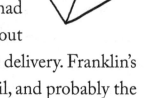 of the tree, Jeffries saw to the letter's delivery. Franklin's parcel was certainly the first Air Mail, and probably the first Underwear Mail, in history.

Undeterred and unembarrassed, both men would fly again. Jean-Pierre actually had a long career of ballooning, until he had a heart attack midair in 1809. After he came crashing back down to earth, his wife, Sophie, took over the family business of aeronautics.

Benjamin Franklin's Whites

During much of the American Revolution, Ben Franklin was living in France as an ambassador. He had been sent to convince King Louis XVI to help America in the war against the British. Desperate to know what he was up to, the British managed to get spies all around him. These secret agents were sending reports about anything they could learn. Even the butler in his Parisian apartment turned out to be a British spy. Franklin kept his secrets very well, though, and the butler-spy had very little to report. One of the very few dispatches sent said only that Franklin's underwear was always clean and "very white." This was probably not the intel the British were looking for.

SHORT SHORT

Thomas Edison's Flying Undies?

As a young man in 1867, Thomas Edison wasn't exactly a model employee. The constant tinkerer was fired from his job as a night shift telegraph operator after burning a hole in his boss's desk with an experiment he was doing on company time. You can imagine the conversation the next morning. Young Tom packed his undies and left town.

By 1879, at the age of 32, Edison's creation of the incandescent lightbulb and phonograph, along with his tendency to never stop experimenting (even if it got him fired) had made him rich and famous. To some, Edison might as well have been a magician because they believed he could make nearly anything a reality.

One London-based magazine called *Punch* decided to have some fun with his inventing ingenuity when they announced "Edison's Anti-Gravity Undergarments." The article, which was clearly a joke, included illustrations of museum visitors examining art hung on the ceiling thanks to their floating undies. Another picture showed parents flying their antigravity diaper–wearing kids like kites. Edison did give the world a lot of cool stuff but, sadly, he never got around to making any flying undies in real life.

Stuck in a Stinky Trunk
Mona Lisa (1503–)

Ask any random person on the street to name a famous painting off the top of their head and they're very likely to say, "Do I know you? Please leave me alone, weirdo!" But if you got lucky and a random street-stroller *did* answer your weird random question, there's a very good chance they would utter two words before they ran away: *Mona Lisa*. Sure, there are other timeless classics of art that would quickly come to the mind of any person you uncomfortably confronted, like Van Gogh's *Starry Night* or Vermeer's *Girl with a Pearl Earring*, but Leonardo DaVinci's portrait of that half-smiling Italian lady is generally regarded as the most famous painting in the world.

Mona Lisa's fame has not always been a given, but it has grown immensely in the last century or so. Unfortunately, the poor painting's path has taken her to many places, exposed her to plenty of people's underclothing, and even gotten her locked inside a trunk with some strange man's socks and underwear. That whole stinky trunk ordeal is actually a big part of how she became as famous as she is today. Once she made it back to the outside, she vaulted from being just another respected Renaissance portrait to becoming a cultural icon that attracts crowds like a bag of stale bread attracts pigeons in the park. Hers may not have been the most direct flight to superstardom, but it sure worked for *Mona Lisa*. Today, she is the most recognized, most visited, and most reproduced painting in history.

Leonardo DaVinci has remained just as famous as his paintings. This is largely thanks to the fact that he was probably more talented than any random roomful of people put together. He is a prime example of a perfect polymath. Without getting into a very wordy, very nerdy definition, *polymath* is a term to describe a person who is super-duper smart and highly accomplished in many different subjects. Many people are really, really good at one specific thing. Other people are pretty good at several different things, but polymaths are really, really good at a lot of different, high-skill subjects.

DaVinci could do just about anything and do it exceedingly well. Among other notable skills, he was a military strategist, a brilliant mathematician, a forward-thinking inventor, a pioneering scientist, and — most famously — an amazing artist.

His path to polymathy wasn't easy, though. Leonardo DaVinci's parents were from different parts of society. One was rich, the other was poor. One was well-connected and the other knew few people with any power. It was a tough way to raise a family, and little left-handed Leo was left in the lurch. His parents offered him no education, despite how much he liked to learn. Luckily, he filled his head with as much knowledge as possible until he found his way into a life-changing apprenticeship. His natural ability with art and amazingly strong grasp of geometry and math (which he somehow learned without ever actually going to school) earned him a spot as an apprentice to an artist in Florence, Italy, named Verrocchio.

At Verrocchio's workshop, Leonardo's first jobs were sweeping the floors and mixing paints, but practically before that paint dried, the youngster was working side by side with his master. You might think Verrocchio lazy, but in reality, he just realized the kid was talented. Learning comes from firsthand experience, so it was common for an apprentice to handle some of the actual painting in such a workshop. Leonardo was no different. Much of the paint painted onto canvases signed by Verrocchio during this time was actually put there by young Leonardo.

In 1472, at only 20 years of age, DaVinci officially became a master himself. This meant he could take on apprentices of his own and — more important — he could accept commissions for his own work, which he started to do as quickly as possible. He quickly learned that, in addition to wearing expensive and luxurious silk underwear beneath their fancy clothes, powerful people often have a thing for buying extravagant creations from nota-ble artists. When Leonardo made a musical instrument called a lute from some precious metal and a dead horse's head for the Duke of Milan, the man was duly impressed, if not a little grossed out.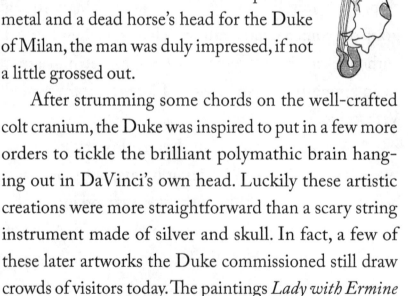

After strumming some chords on the well-crafted colt cranium, the Duke was inspired to put in a few more orders to tickle the brilliant polymathic brain hang-ing out in DaVinci's own head. Luckily these artistic creations were more straightforward than a scary string instrument made of silver and skull. In fact, a few of these later artworks the Duke commissioned still draw crowds of visitors today. The paintings *Lady with Ermine* (which is a portrait of a woman in fancy clothes remain-ing incredibly calm while cradling a live weasel) and *The*

Last Supper (which was painted on a wall that was later used for target practice by Napoleon's army) are some of Leonardo's most famous and enduring works of art[3].

But it's easy to make the case that the *Mona Lisa*, which he started painting in 1503, is the most famous piece of art Leonardo ever created. This is interesting, because some people disagree about who Mona Lisa actually was. The best guess is that she was the wife of a silk merchant named Francesco Del Giocondo. As a silk merchant in Florence, there's a decent chance that this man kept the wealthy people of Florence in full supply of sundries like soft silk for their fancy undies. It's even more likely that he hired DaVinci to immortalize his wife by painting her likeness on a wooden board. His wife's name was Lisa Gherardini. Unfortunately, a seatbelt was nowhere in DaVinci's list of inventions. Lisa could have used one, because she[4] was about to take quite a ride.

Of course, the ride was slow at first. The poor lady spent hours sitting on her rear, fighting boredom and trying to hold a smile for Leonardo as his brush slowly painted her image. After all of the sitting and holding still, DaVinci sent her home empty-handed. The artist couldn't stop working on the painting. Years later, he still

---

[3] No thanks to Napoleon.
[4] Ok, really just her likeness.

claimed not to be finished. In the end, Francesco and Lisa would *never* get the painting they asked – *and paid* – for.

As Leonardo shuffled around Italy looking for patronage, he packed up the *Mona Lisa* — along with his outer clothes, underclothes, books, and tools — and took the painting wherever the wind blew him. Did he do this because he had grown so attached? Because he wasn't satisfied and needed to work on the portrait further? Because he felt it could be his greatest masterpiece? We don't know. But we do know that he took it with him to France when King François I invited him to live and work there under his patronage. The *Mona Lisa* was still in

DaVinci's possession when he died in 1519, which was a full 16 years after he was hired to paint poor Lisa Gherardini del Giocondo. She was probably wondering where her portrait was.

Lisa would never cast her eyes upon the painting again. DaVinci left it to his assistant, who promptly sold the painting to King François of France. As an art-loving royal, François could afford surrounding himself with the finest paintings and sculptures. Also thanks to his royal fortunes, he could afford several gigantic homes, each of which he stuffed to the gills with incredible art meant to impress anyone lucky enough to walk in. For years he hung *Mona Lisa* on the wall of one of these royal homes. There is reason to believe that for a period of time it hung in his bathroom.

It remained in royal hands for over two centuries after that, until the French Revolution of the late 1700s. This was when the citizens of France rebelled against the idea of kings and queens, along with their unchecked power and wealth (and private art collections, it would appear). When King-at-the-time Louis XVI and his wife Marie Antoinette were overthrown and then thrown into graves in their underwear, the *royal* art collection became a *public* art collection. This was the birth of the Louvre as a museum and it soon became a place the public could see all of the art that once belonged to the French monarchy. There, on a wall amongst an immense, newly public collection, was *Mona Lisa*.

However, the new French Republic that gave power to the people didn't really take the first go-round. Just a few years later, a man named Napoleon came to power in France and he eventually ruled as an emperor rather than an elected president. He was a military genius with a thirst for land, power, and, as it would turn out, portraits of bored-looking women painted by Italians. She might not have stood out to many people, but something about her spoke to the new leader of France. Emperor Napoleon Bonaparte took the *Mona Lisa* off the wall at the museum and hung it in his bedroom. If the real Lisa could have somehow seen through the painted eyes of her portrait, she would have undoubtedly seen one of history's most famous and powerful men in his underwear.

Emperors are mortal, though. They come and go like anyone else. Paintings, on the other hand, can fare much better than a human, if properly cared for. A century later, Napoleon  was a just another body in a grave while *Mona Lisa* was once again enjoying the care and attention her cozy old home in The Louvre offered. Museum security figured her new spot on the wall would keep her a safe distance from anyone else's underwear from then on. Were they right? They were worse than right. *They were wrong.* Napoleon wasn't the last person to pluck her from her perch on the wall and condemn her to a private residence far away from the eyes of the public.

One Tuesday morning in 1911, a man made his way through The Louvre to visit the *Mona Lisa*. He was a museum regular who painted passable copies of notable paintings to sell to tourists. The *Mona Lisa* definitely wasn't the star of the show at the museum, but he still occasionally spent the day recreating the portrait which never seemed to satisfy DaVinci. Plans for his day of duplicating DaVinci's details were upended by what he saw — or rather, didn't see. Instead of Lisa's semi-smiling face, he found nothing but a bare wall and the nails where Lisa should have hung. The alarm was raised. She was gone.

Soon, investigators were combing all of Paris trying to find the vanished DaVinci. Needing to look at the crime from all angles, they even confronted famous painter Pablo Picasso. It wasn't as absurd of an accusation as you might think — he did have some small statues in his home that had been pilfered from The Louvre, but the man was *Mona Lisa*-less. Officials were left with little to go on, and the case of the missing *Mona Lisa* became international news. People who had never even heard of *Mona Lisa* were now following the story as officials looked high and low, questioned collectors and criminals, yet still came up empty-handed.

People were perplexed about how a painting could just be plucked from the wall and promenaded straight out the door to the populated streets of Paris. Even more disconcerting to them was how it just disappeared. The *Mona Lisa* was quickly becoming the most famous painting in the world, thanks to the fact that *no one knew where she was*. For nearly two years she remained missing.

The man who boldly artnapped the poor painting did not think she belonged in France. Vincenzo Peruggia was his name, and he was mistaken about one big matter. Peruggia did not realize that King François had purchased the portrait. Instead, he wrongfully assumed that Napoleon had stolen it from Italy to hang in his bedroom. The truth would have mattered little to him, though. His only belief was that Italy, the home of both DaVinci and the real Lisa, was the painting's rightful home. Since Vincent was an Italian living in Paris — *who happened to work at the Louvre* — he felt he was in a unique position to right this wrong.

While working as maintenance man at the museum, he regularly cast his eyes upon the very painting he would hide from the rest of the world, likely fuming with anger that the masterwork was not on Italian soil. He took matters (and the painting) into his own hands early one morning when the museum was closed to the public. It's believed he and a couple of accomplices spent the night in a cramped closet, awoke to pull the painting from the wall, and then walked right out the museum's door.

Of course, trying to conceal the rigid and awkwardly-sized artwork as he walked through the galleries was difficult. The best Vincenzo could do was stick it underneath his smock. It's a wonder another maintenance man he encountered didn't notice the rectangular protrusion, but perhaps that man simply wanted nothing to do with whatever appeared to be going on under Peruggia's clothes.

Soon, like all the other museum workers, Peruggia was visited by detectives trying to find any clue to the whereabouts of the disappearing DaVinci. Amazingly, they didn't realize that the *Mona Lisa* was under the very table where they sat as they questioned him in his tiny Parisian apartment. Despite throwing them off the trail, Peruggia realized there was too much attention around the now world-famous *Mona Lisa*. It would have been foolish to try to turn it over to Italy at this point, so he shared the cramped quarters of his dingy apartment with *Mona Lisa* for almost two years. No one who knew the mustached man would suspect what treasured company he kept.

Finally, in 1913, Peruggia began communicating with an Italian art dealer about a valuable painting he wanted to find a home for in Italy. When they met, the dealer solemnly watched as Peruggia opened his steamer trunk to reveal not a DaVinci, but his socks and underwear instead. With no apparent shame, the thief pulled out these unmentionables, along with a few other insignificant objects, and threw them on the table. As he gazed at these "wretched belongings," the dealer probably began regretting the meeting. With a hint of despair and the aroma of stale clothes in his nose, he peered into what appeared to be an empty trunk. It was then that Peruggia reached in and pulled up a false bottom hiding the artwork. If the woman in the portrait had  been real, she would have gratefully gasped the fresh air. Instead, the gasp of relief came from the art dealer. Safe and sound, out came the purloined portrait. The *Mona Lisa* had been found in good shape, despite her extended stay in a box with undies.

Suspecting something fishy about the situation (beyond the stench of Peruggia's laundry), the art dealer had alerted authorities in advance. Once the *Mona Lisa* was verified to be the real portrait, Vincenzo Peruggia was quickly arrested for his theft. Word spread around the world that *Mona Lisa*, now probably the most well-known painting in the world, had been recovered. Italian officials pledged to return her to the perch on the wall at the Louvre, in France.

After serving a shockingly light sentence of seven months for the international crime, Peruggia enlisted to serve with the Italian army during World War I. Then, demonstrating the same lack of shame for his crime that he did for sharing his undies with an art dealer, he had the gall to move back to Paris and open a paint shop. Some of his Parisian customers might have used the pigments purchased from Peruggia to paint copies of the very same pilfered painting that had once shared his apartment.

Of course, the *Mona Lisa* outlived him, as she'll hopefully do with any other human who crosses her path. But thanks to the stinky trunk ordeal, more people than ever learned about the painting. As a result, everyone wanted to see her face.

This trend has continued in the century following Peruggia's crime. Lisa's face is everywhere today. You could say she's larger than life, which is why many people who make the pilgrimage to stand in front of the portrait are surprised to find it's quite small — only the size of an average computer screen. Still, she is visited by millions of curious tourists every year. Lessons have been learned and today her security detail is drastically improved. It is everyone's hope to keep her as far away as possible from anyone else's underwear, or anything else.

BRA

A 19-year-old Mary Phelps Jacob dreaded the idea of attending yet another formal social event, which always required her to squeeze into to the "boxlike armor of whalebone and pink cordage," as she described her corset. It was 1910, and she was not alone in loathing the suffocating, torturous contraption.

So she called for a needle, thread, ribbon, and two handkerchiefs. Minutes later, she put on her invention — a bra. It brought great relief. Word of her ingenuity must have gotten around, because that night at the ball, woman after woman curiously approached her, wondering if they could have one, too. When a stranger offered her money to make one, a light bulb went off in Phelps's mind: She should get into the bra business.

To be fair, other bras existed prior to this, but hers was unique and universal. Its adjustability meant it would easily work for anyone and gave women the freedom to be active without restricting movement. Try playing tennis in a corset!

Phelps was awarded a patent for her "backless brassiere" in 1914, and opened a business in Boston soon after. Never making as much as she hoped, she sold the patent and turned her attention to other things, namely book publishing. The firm to whom she sold the patent made a tidy fortune. Her bra design turned out to be perfect for the changing fashions of the time, when women were throwing out their restrictive clothing in the name of comfort and ease. It's believed they made millions of dollars as a result. But she didn't miss out on every opportunity. Later in life, working under the name of Caresse Crosby, she helped publish the early works of writers like Henry Miller, Anais Nin, and Ernest Hemingway, before they were famous.

Mermaid in Stockings

Annette Kellerman (1886–1975)

In the late 1800s, people began jumping into the water as they never had before. We're not talking about daring dives and flailing flops, here. Modern moves like the cannonball, can opener, and flying squirrel had yet to be perfected. But, for the first time, more and different people were dipping more than just their toes into the waters of the world. Of course, the refreshing pleasure of a nice float had been known to many though the ages, but around this time, swimming was finally becoming the popular pastime and hobby it is today. Far beyond the joy of splashing in the surf, people began to realize that swimming was as healthy as it was enjoyable.

When Annette Kellerman[5] was born in New South Wales, Australia, in 1886, it didn't look like she'd be one of those many new swimmers. As a young girl she had a very difficult time walking. Doctors did not agree on what caused her ailment. Some said it was polio, but others thought it was rickets. Whatever the case was, her legs could not support her body. At the age of six, she was fitted for metal leg braces to help her walk. For years, the young girl met all of her challenges with the additional support of her parents, who could see her determination as clearly as they could see the waves break on the nearby beach. When a clever new doctor recommended the young girl start swimming, they saw the wisdom, found a swim teacher, and practically threw her into the water.

This prescription might have been the most momentous doctor's order in history. Swimming allowed Annette to develop the muscles in her legs, thanks to the physical freedom of floating. Slowly the strength came, and within a few short years Annette was usually seen walking to the tidal swimming pools of Sydney Harbor with comfort, ease, and a look of water-loving excitement on her face. Her staunch determination was no surprise, but the teenager's growing speed and dexterity in the water

---

[5] Sometimes her name was spelled Kellermann, and sometimes it was spelled Kellerman. I'm choosing to use the spelling with a single *n* because it will save ink.

certainly caught people's attention. Even more surprising was the discovery that the young woman had a fierce competitive streak.

The supportive metal braces became a rusty memory which rarely bothered her mind. Instead, a mere decade later, Annette was completely focused on swimming as fast and as far as she could. There were not many women in competitive swimming at the time, so she knew there was room at the top for her. Her first goal was to set a world record in the pool. It didn't take long. At the age of 16, she swam the 100m faster than any woman ever had before. It was remarkable for anyone, but especially for a young woman who had struggled to walk less than 10 years before.

The waves seemed to part and Annette began to see a clear path for her future. Most lives are lived on land, but she seemed to know that her greatest moments would take place in the water. So she dove in. It was more than just the thrill of swimming fast and winning a match that tickled her toes, though. Annette truly treasured her time treading pools, diving into lakes, or splashing in the ocean. The pruned fingers, limbered limbs, and pleasant exhaustion after a day in the water left her feeling delighted, and she wanted other people to be dripping with the same joy.

This doesn't mean she was without a few criticisms for the sport. At the top of the list of things she wished to change about swimming were women's swimsuits.

If you were to challenge someone to make the most uncomfortable or most dangerous swimsuit imaginable, they might get pretty close to something that women actually wore in the late 1800s. One of society's biggest concerns at the time was how a woman dressed. Dull opinions from nosy people were quite common, and many of these nosiest believed *just because a woman was heading to the beach for a fun day of frolicking in the surf, sand, and sun, she had no right to relax her dress code!* These same nosy people pointed incredulously to the scandalous new bloomers women were so proud to tromp around in on land. The full-length, loose-fitting underpants were freeing for a day's walk, but when women were expected to adapt the full under-wear combo for swimming, the ensemble proved to be quite a hindrance. The woman had more to contend with than just the bloomers; she was also covered from neck to knees by a dress.

As if the idea of swimming in a dress and leg-length underwear wasn't bad enough, consider that many of those waterlogged dresses were made of wool. When wet, wool weighs an awful lot. As a result, many of those wool-wearing women went straight to the bottom of the water. And just in case the hemline of a woolen dress scandalously rose above a lady's knees as she swam, some suits even had metal weights sewn into the bottom of the fabric. The modesty-minded and heavy-handed alteration helped keep the dress down, along with the poor lady's spirits (not to mention, her entire body if she wasn't a strong swimmer).

Obviously, this was not going to work for Annette. Watching men swim carefree and unhindered would certainly make a lady wonder why she couldn't wear the safe and speedy swimsuits they enjoyed. There's a saying: *Sometimes it's better to beg for forgiveness rather than ask for permission.* The saying might have crossed Annette's mind when she first put on a men's suit instead of her own. In most places in the world, people would expect permission — or an apology — for such a bold move by a lady, but Annette got — or gave — neither. She just did it.

It may have caused an immediate uproar and it may have ultimately changed the fashion of swimwear, but, more important to Annette, a men's suit was faster and safer. As many women had learned, a poor suit could take the joy out of swimming and make it difficult — even dangerous. The decision to don a new suit would slowly change both the world and the typical family beach trip.

Everyone can agree that drowning at the beach tends to put a damper on one's vacation.

By today's standards, Annette's new suit was pretty tame. Really, it was just a tank top connected to a pair of shorts ending just above the knees. It fit her body closely, and that was by design. Extra flowing fabric meant slower swimming, and Annette had records to break. Still, some folks found it simply scandalous.

The strong reactions helped her get attention when she decided to take the new suit to Europe. There was plenty of curiosity about her new un-weighted, dress-free, and drowning-resistant swimsuit, but more than that, everyone wanted to see if she lived up to her reputation as the world's most incredible swimmer.

She did not disappoint. For crowds of spectators, Annette added marathon swims of the Thames and Seine Rivers to her growing resume. These certainly weren't pleasure swims. Tugboats and barges chugged along beside her, turning up wake in the oily, dirty water. Despite the sludge, newspapers published stories of the "Australian Mermaid" and her river excursions to the interest of everyone.

Looking for a big story to cover, one paper hired her to swim across the English Channel. This was the same stretch of salty water separating England and France that two nearly-naked aeronauts had ballooned over in the previous century (see Chapter 5). Annette loved the challenge and attention, so she slipped into her suit, slathered herself in seal grease, and set out swimming. She wasn't  alone. In addition to the boats trailing her for safety, several men were attempting the arduous crossing themselves. Also covered in grease, the men had the additional aerodynamic luxury of swimming while completely naked.

The ocean water was too much for her (and for all of the men, too). After six hours of swimming and making it past the halfway point, she had to signal the safety boats to get her out. Later, she'd say her endurance was up to the challenge, but she was not physically strong enough for the rough water. The official report chalked the failure up to seasickness. Whatever queasiness she felt was probably a result of being surrounded by greasy naked guys rather than the sloshy roller coaster of ocean waves.

Always eager for an audience, she turned to the stage. Vaudeville entertainment was a huge draw for people at the time, and crowds flocked to the theaters to see variety shows filled with music, dance, comedy, and — believe it or not — swimming. Taking advantage of her growing popularity in Europe, Annette joined the bill of some large shows. Performing a mermaid act in a gigantic tank that was wheeled onto the stage, she blended ballet, diving, and synchronized swimming into a popular production that captured imaginations and raked in ticket sales.

The royal family of England, as curious as everyone, wished to see Annette's performance. The invitation probably came as a shock to Annette. The little girl from Australia was now the most famous swimmer in the world and would be performing *on request* for the most powerful people in England.

If the request didn't come as a surprise, the second part of the invitation certainly did. The royal family was very proper and traditionally commanded the strictest standards of etiquette. Anyone in their presence had to be very careful with what they did and what they said. Beyond behavior, people in their presence also had to be careful with what they wore. It didn't matter if they were at a banquet table or in a giant fish tank. Annette was informed that her suit was improper, so she would need to cover her bare legs in the presence of royalty.

Annette pondered the dilemma. It would be impossible to do her act well in a weighted, woolen, woman-drowning dress. She'd either die or disappoint the royal family (I mean, they'd be disappointed if she couldn't swim well in an unfamiliar suit, but hopefully they'd be more disappointed if she drowned). To solve the problem, she went to her underwear drawer.

It's easy to believe Annette spent all of her time swimming, getting as pruney as an Australian raisin, but she did spend at least some of her time walking around on the dry ground like the rest of us. For these rare times above the surface, she wore dresses, blouses, and all of the usual things women of the time wore. Underneath those landlubber dresses, she often wore stockings. It was a pair of these thick black stockings that would save her performance.

By sewing the hosiery into the short legs of the knee-length swimsuit, Annette created a one-piece that stretched from her toes to her shoulders, offering enough coverage to appease the sensitive eyes of the royal family and yet enough mobility to still swim like the mermaid those royals wished to see. The underwear modification was a brilliant solution and she was a hit with the noble audience.

After conquering Europe in such grand fashion, Annette looked for the next great adventure. She cast her un-goggled Australian eyes towards America. It might have come as a surprise, but dealing with society's expectations wouldn't be much easier across the ocean. What should have been a casual swim one day at Revere Beach, not far from Boston, turned into a new scandal. Believing she was no longer in need of the stockings, she brought out her original suit and readied herself for some bare-legged bathing in the Atlantic Ocean. Before she could even dip the tiniest tip of her toes in the foam, she felt a tap on her shoulder. It was the police.

Annette was arrested for indecent exposure. In the eyes of the arresting officer, swimming in her suit was the same as swimming in her underwear. Some folks think the whole thing might have been a publicity stunt. Annette was a pretty big star, and Revere Beach was well-known for having overeager cops enforcing a stringent dress code. Whatever the case might have been, she made her own case to the judge when she explained that her suit was safer, easier, and as proper as any man's. The judge knew she was right. He requested that she wear a robe while relaxing on Revere Beach, but made it clear that she was welcome to swim in her suit, free from legal intervention.

If it was a publicity stunt, it worked, because the incident got a lot of attention. Before long, women all over the world were wearing similar swimsuits, which they called Annette Kellermans.

The rest of Annette's life was dedicated to her core beliefs, and she wrote best-selling books about swimming, health, and fitness. She appeared in a few motion pictures, and later in her life she owned one of the earliest health food stores in California.

It was a remarkable life, and her impact is felt with every women's swimsuit hanging on store shelves or stuffed into suitcases and swim bags. It's easy to argue that her biggest break came with an invite from England's royal family, which she couldn't have fulfilled without the black stockings she found in her underwear drawer.

Margery Booth, Underwear Spy

Margery Booth could hit a high note with the best of them, even when facing life-or-death circumstances. The British opera singer moved to her husband's native Germany in the 1930s and built a great reputation on her powerful voice. Her career hit a bit of a snag when World War II began, but she soon found herself performing in prisoner of war camps. Foolishly, the Nazi government trusted her to be around British soldiers they had captured. Margery did what any self-respecting British opera singer would do: she became a spy against Hitler and his government.

Once, she sang in front of Hitler and his cronies while carrying secret messages. Just before taking the stage, she hid the documents in her underwear. Had she been caught, she would have most certainly been executed. The Nazis did not take well to underwear-smuggling spies, but Margery didn't even break a sweat. She sang so well that night, she got an ovation from the very man she was playing for a fool.

Hitler sent her flowers while she sent her secret messages to British agents.

Civil War Smugglers

During the American Civil War, women on both sides of the conflict were eager to help. However, it was difficult because few women at the time had any sort of political power. So, while some chose to care for the sick and wounded as nurses in the field, others found more creative ways to influence the war's outcome.

Famously, many women secretly lived as men while serving in the army, and often acted as spies for their side. Other women chose not to don a scratchy woolen army uniform, but instead sought a solution in the giant hoop skirts they were probably already wearing. The space between a woman's body and the protruding fabric of the big bell-shaped outfits made for a perfect place to hide all sorts of things from the prying eyes of enemies.

In an effort to help their armies, sneaky Civil War women secretly stashed things such as weapons, boots, clothing, money, coded messages, and more underneath gigantic skirts. Many were successful in delivering their clandestine contraband, but not every undisclosed under-clothes undertaking was a success. One Southern woman, named Rose O'Neal Greenhow, certainly came to regret secretly sewing gold onto the inside of her hoopskirt. When she fell into the ocean trying to escape pursuers, she was pulled underwater by the weight of the metal.

Let this be a lesson to you: It's a bad idea to swim in a hoopskirt — and an even worse one to carry heavy metal if you do. So when you go to the pool, always leave your gold at home.

Hanging By a Thread

John Wesley Powell (1834–1902)

There are a lot of dead people in Arlington National Cemetery. That is pretty normal for a graveyard. But as America's most famous cemetery, Arlington also attracts hundreds of living people every day. Here's the thing, though: if a zombie apocalypse were to ever happen, Arlington would most certainly be the worst place to find yourself. Because it's filled with many of America's toughest people, the place would be crawling with some equally fearsome zombies. Plan any visits wisely.

The place isn't just filled with soldier zombies-to-be, though. Under other gravestones, visitors would find the mouldering bodies of United States presidents, the bones of a few astronauts, as well as the remains of a one-armed man named John Wesley Powell. The epitaph on his headstone reads:

1834–1902
Soldier, Explorer, Scientist

Powell's life story of narrow misses and incredible escapes is hard to fit in a book, let alone a waist-high stone marker. The guy was lucky he made it to 1902. It could have easily ended for him back in 1869, while he was risking his rear end for science. If not for one particularly important pair of underwear, not only would he have died, but his body would have been lost completely. He certainly would not have enjoyed the honor of eternity in America's most hallowed ground.

Instead, poor John Wesley would've slowly deteriorated in the blazing western sun, been gobbled up by Grand Canyon creatures, or been carried away like a capsized canoe on the Colorado River. He owed a lot to that pair of underwear, which is remarkable — since they weren't even his underwear.

Powell was born in New York to parents who were the good kind of troublemakers. His father was an abolitionist, which meant he worked to end slavery in America. Not everyone agreed with him, and his outspoken beliefs created constant conflict with neighbors. Thanks to angry mobs at their doorstep, the family was forced to pack up and leave several times in the middle of the night. Each time, they headed farther west. After New York, they fled Ohio. Then the family was chased out of Wisconsin, only to finally settle down in Illinois.

John liked learning when he first started school in Ohio, but the local kids never took kindly to him. He believed this was because their families disagreed with the elder Mr. Powell's views on slavery. Once John Wesley had to sprint for the safety of home while the bullies on his trail hurled sticks, stones, and hurtful words.

Rather than send him back to school, his parents hired a private tutor. It was a momentous (and lucky) decision. Not only was the tutor a great teacher, but his house was a mini-museum filled with fossils, arrowheads, mineral samples, and more.

In the 1800s, Earth was a big blue ball of mystery. People just didn't know much about it, and science was still developing as a field of study. John and his teacher would be among the curious few genuinely searching and studying in hopes of determining Earth's true age. Many believed our planet was only hundreds, or perhaps thousands, of years old. John Wesley Powell's teacher reasoned it was actually millions of years old. Today, we know it's even older than that, but at least he was thinking in the right direction, using evidence and a thoughtful mind to support his beliefs. Learning to think this way changed the world for John Wesley Powell.

The teacher recognized a natural curiosity in John, and together they spent many hours poring over books, maps, and specimens. Often they'd get dirty poking around riverbanks or dense forests to see what interesting things they could uncover. When he started college, John found himself pretty bored with what the professors were teaching. On the subject of science, he had already learned more than most of the teachers knew. So he dropped out and floated down the river in a boat.

He wasn't in any rush on this trip. Every single day he would park his boat on the bank, take off his shoes, roll up his pant legs, and plop his bare feet deep in the mud. When his toes felt the rough ridges of a mussel deep in the muck, it was brought to the surface and excitedly added to his growing collection. John Wesley wasn't a braggart, but his mussel collection was known to be the finest mussel collection in 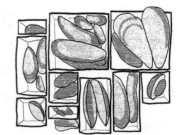 the United States — if you're into that sort of thing. John was definitely into it. Unfortunately he had to leave his massive mussel shell collection behind (along with his new, mussel-indifferent wife) when the Civil War began.

When Lincoln made the call for troops in 1861, Powell was among the first to join. "It was a great thing to destroy slavery," he wrote. The mud-loving brainiac was a good soldier, and his talents lent themselves well to map-making. Making sense of the land was valuable for the Union army officers, but he soon also became a leader on the battlefield. Eventually he earned an artillery command of his own.

Despite the horrors of war, he never lost his curiosity. If his men were digging trenches or earthworks, he would often follow behind, scouring the upturned earth for more fossils to add to his collection.

At the famous Battle of Shiloh, he lost his arm. A minié ball, fired from a Confederate rifle, smashed into him as he was signaling an order to his troops. Like the arms and legs of many soldiers, the appendage was amputated, tossed in a gruesome, bloody pile, and soon forgotten about. While many mourned the loss of their long-gone limbs, Powell only looked towards the future. Before long he was back in the battlefield, where he stayed for the remainder of the war.

When the war ended, Powell grew bored and restless. He worked as a teacher but quickly realized he was not cut out for the four walls of a classroom. As the years went by, his itch for adventure only grew itchier. It seemed like the itch was always just out of the reach of his one hand.

With maniacal enthusiasm, he told people of his dream to conquer the Grand Canyon. Understandably, they were flabbergasted. No one of European descent had successfully descended the gargantuan and turbulent Grand Canyon, and now a one-armed man was going to try? They wished him luck and then laughed behind his back.

The more he thought about it, the more excited he got. The Colorado River had flowed through the stony landscape for eons, and the constant power of the water eroded the earth, leaving deep cuts and towering walls. Nowhere else was there such an opportunity. To the trained eyes of Powell, seeing these features up close would be like gazing into a hidden history of the planet. All of his life he had pondered the mysteries and learned more about America's geology than nearly any other person alive. So it made perfect sense in his mind. He'd take a crew of men down the river, draw some maps, observe the deep cuts in the earth for clues, and spend hours on the steep shores and steeper walls of the canyon, collecting specimens for deeper study.

He hired a team of men and bought some big, clunky boats, which were not ideal for the journey. To make things worse, the men had to paddle backwards, blind to the rocks and twists the  river constantly delivered. On the rapids, these skiffs would toss their bodies around like tennis balls in a clothes dryer. In order to keep himself out of the water, he mounted a cleat to the floor of the lead boat, to which he tied a rope. While riding, John Wesley would lean back with his weight and hold the rope  tightly with his one arm. Sometimes he was able to stand up, but usually, like all the others, he bounced, bobbed, and bashed around the boat.

After committing to the heavy boats, Powell did anything else he could to travel light. Bringing enough bacon and flour to feed the flock of hungry explorers for weeks on end was the main concern. So after the bulky food was packed, Powell tucked a select few scientific instruments and packets of writing paper into the boat's bits of bacon-free space. Weight and mobility would be an issue on the river rapids, so he insisted the crew carry little else. Despite this, one of his men suggested bringing a few pairs of red flannel long underwear for everyone on the mission. This idea struck Powell as a good one. The underwear would be warm on cold nights and wouldn't add too much weight, so permission was granted. The leader probably never considered the many other uses for a nice pair of long johns, but one day soon he would thank his lucky stars for making the right decision.

Each man left with several pairs, but faster than you can say "itchy flannel in the summer sun," most of their carefully packed stuff was gone. The boats rarely made it through a day remaining upright. Overturned boats regularly sent the paper, bacon, and some of the underwear floating down the river, never to return.

Before entering the canyon, the river water was pretty smooth and easy. However, when they reached the gurgling, rocky rapids, the men realized it was pointless to even bother with outer clothes. Sure, the soaking wet fabric was uncomfortable, but when they were inevitably flung from the boat, the extra weight made drowning more likely. So they ditched their clothes in the name of safety, finding it was easier to just row in their underwear. They would have been quite a sight to see, if anyone had been around to see them, but the Grand Canyon was not the tourist destination it is today. The boatloads of wet, smelly men in their underwear crashed into nearly every rock in the wild river for miles and miles.

Just as he had been during the war, Powell was fearless. Nothing stood between him and his goals. The whole reason for the trip, why everyone was risking their lives, was to learn all they could about the exposed earth of the canyon. Each new specimen was important to Powell's research, so he would do nearly anything. He was the kind of boss who led by example. Luckily, his men were paying attention.

One day, after hours of exhausting work trying (and failing) to dodge river rocks, Powell and a man named Bradley decided to explore the steep cliffs looming above their heads. With two legs and an arm, Powell daringly scaled the face of the rock wall. The equally brave Bradley led the way, remaining just above Powell as they pulled themselves higher and higher. The climb was going well for the pair until, 800 feet above the ground, Powell found himself with very little to grab ahold of. He did not panic, but it was very clear that he had become stuck on a narrow, rocky shelf. The not-so-dependable tree root in his hand was the only thing keeping him from tumbling backwards to his doom on the rock-hard ground far below.

Remaining as calm as he could, his eyes scanned around his perch for a way to scramble to safety. There was nothing he could do. Powell realized he had chosen a terrible path and there was little hope. Most people would agree: this should've been the end of Powell. It was no Arlington cemetery, but, as far as final resting places go, the spot had its own special beauty.

Fortunately, his climbing partner had taken a different path and made it to a perch safely over Powell's head. Bradley's face peered down from above but it brought no relief. No matter how Bradley stretched and strained his arms, Powell was out of his reach. With their muscles fatigued and aching already from a hard day of rowing, both men realized they were running out of time. Powell couldn't hold on much longer. Quick thinking led the men to one conclusion: The only way out of this pickle would require Bradley to take off his long underwear.

Now, naked on the narrow ledge of a rock wall high above the river, Bradley hid any signs of birthday suit embarrassment. In his hands he held his red flannel long underwear, which he hoped would be stout enough to pull Powell from the perilous predicament. He dangled the long-john lifeline over the ledge until one of the legs hung near Powell's hand, which was tightly clasped onto the tree root keeping him from falling. Powell took a breath, let go, and grabbed the undies at the very instant he began to fall. To both men's relief, the underwear held. With a steady tick-tock motion, Bradley was able to pull Powell to safety on the ledge beside him.

It didn't take Powell long to recover from the ordeal. Unfazed by staring down death and defeating it with dirty underwear, he was eager to get back to work. He may have failed to fully appreciate his role in the most harrowing underwear rescue in recorded history. He thanked his naked friend and went back to digging fossils. The rest of the trip was long and difficult, but luckily the remaining long johns were only used for keeping warm in the cold canyon nights.

Powell made many important discoveries on the journey, which he used to fill in the gaps of his under-standing of Earth's natural history. As a scientist, his discoveries made an impact still felt today. He was also one of the first to realize that Amer-  ica's plans for settling the western part of the continent would be complicated by the lack of fresh water. Despite his warning, little action was taken. Still today, water supply is a problem in many western states.

Powell returned a few years later to complete a second Grand Canyon journey. This time he brought plenty of rope.

Union Suit

Is there anything more classic than a bright-red, flannel, one-piece garment covering everything from the ankles to the wrists? Add a trapdoor with buttons on the rear end and you've got some practical, pure gold underwear. Speaking of precious ore, you might even picture a scruffy prospector mining for that pure gold when you think of the union suit. These comedically perfect coveralls, however, were originally born out of the same dress reform that gave women the world-changing wearables called bloomers.

Patented in 1868 and initially called "emancipation union under flannel," the union suit was a full-bodied alternative to the uncomfortable and stifling clothing many women wore under their cumbersome dresses. Because the flannel coverings were so warm and conveniently mobile, men soon started wearing them, too.

Today, it's easy to think the name came from the Union army during the American Civil War, which ended in 1865. It is more likely that the term "union" was actually in reference to how the top and bottom were joined together in one big lengthy pair of long johns. This union of unflashy fabric fast became a favorite for all. In the decades that followed, hundreds of thousands of union suits were sold, worn — and occasionally laundered.

It was common for people to wear the flannel undies for a full winter season without taking them off once. This is not recommended, but if you find something you love, there's nothing wrong with sticking with it. Just make sure you've got an access hatch for the times when nature calls.

God Save the Queen's Undies

Queen Victoria (1819–1901)

Imagine being awoken by your mother in the dim darkness of an early morning. With no explanation, and no chance to cover your wrinkled dressing gown, you're taken to a room full of prim and proper men with titles like Lord Conyngham and Archbishop of Canterbury. Blinking your groggy eyes, wearing only your underclothes, and wondering if you're dreaming, you hear the most important news of your life.

What might sound like some kind of weird knickers-nightmare was real life for Victoria of England. The poor young lady was in her underwear when she found out she would be the queen.

It was an overwhelming thing to hear at the crack of dawn. The 18-year-old was suddenly in control of the British Empire, the most powerful empire in the world. Considering this, they could've given her time to get dressed, maybe even have a cup of coffee. It wasn't even really an emergency. Everyone knew that her uncle, King William, was going to die. In fact, as his lights were dimming, he spitefully told Victoria's mom (whom he loathed) that he would wait to die until Victoria turned 18. That way, Victoria would be queen and wouldn't have to share any power with her unpleasant mother.

It seems like a hard promise to make — you're not always in control of your expiration date — but somehow Uncle Will kept his word and died in 1837, one month after Victoria's eighteenth birthday. As a result, the weight of the crown came to rest solely upon on Victoria's bed head that morning. Hopefully the archbishop and other stuffy men let her put some proper clothes on before they actually put it there.

Prior to the crowning, Victoria's childhood was far from picturesque. Being a princess might sound awesome, but a royal birth (and the incredible wealth that often comes along with it) doesn't always equate to happiness.

Her grandfather was King George III. He was the guy who had to deal not just with George Washington and the rebelling Americans, but also the power-hungry French military genius Napoleon. Those are some serious enemies, so it's easy to understand why, at the end of his life, there wasn't much of his brain left in good working order. Even though he bumbled around the castle in confusion in his later years, he did have four sons, so at least the throne seemed safe. Unfortunately, two of them, including Victoria's dad, died. The other two of Victoria's uncles would both sit on the throne for a while, but neither had an heir, so when they also wound up dead and buried, Victoria was next in line. Knowing this would eventually happen, her mom controlled the girl's life with an iron fist.

Victoria's mom devised the Kensington System, a ridiculously strict set of rules for raising her daughter. One of the biggest commands was that Victoria was never to be left alone. She slept every single night in the same bed as her mother. Despite the lack of privacy, the number of people she could see was small. There were only two children she was  allowed to play with, and, at all costs, she was kept away from her kingly uncle (along with pretty much any other adult who might put any sort of ideas in her head). From the day she was born until the day she became queen, she almost never left Kensington Palace.

While many people have found the responsibilities and trappings of a royal crown restrictive and stressful, it actually brought a bit of freedom into Victoria's life. As the queen, she could tell her unpleasant mom (and anyone else) to beat it. For once in her life, she could go where she wished, do as she liked, and begin to immerse herself in the work of ruling. Of course, it would turn out that ruling an empire is harder than most people think.

As with most young royals, everyone was concerned with finding her a suitable husband. She was a pleasant-mannered, attractive young queen, so matrimonial overtures were sung from the lips of what seemed like every random man in the British Empire. Probably enjoying the freedom she had craved for so long, Victoria remained single for the first several years of her reign. In the end, she did what so many other royals have done: she married a cousin.

Around the time her cousin-husband Albert entered her life, an uninvited boy weaseled his way in as well. Buckingham Palace, where the royal couple lived, left a lot to be desired when it came to security. It was a grubby little fellow known as the Boy Jones who would make this painfully clear. He had no business being inside Buckingham Palace, but he had a passion for sneaking in just the same.

Newspaper accounts simply described the kid as "dirty." Because he was small and his face was covered in grime, people assumed he was a chimneysweep, like so many other boys his size and age. It made sense because most assumed that the intruder snuck in through the extensive chimney and flue system. The Boy Jones was probably just dirty because he didn't take many baths. He may have hid in fireplaces, but he certainly didn't need chimneys to get in.

Foolishly, people of the palace thought nothing of leaving a few windows and doors unlocked at the queen's quarters. The Boy Jones was always on the lookout for a good opportunity, and one day an unattended, open service door was an invitation he couldn't turn down. Once he darted inside, his dark filthy clothes and grubby  face became perfect camouflage in the lightless rooms of the palace. For hours he frolicked around, completely undetected.

It was nighttime when his dirty face finally surprised a poor guard named William Cox, who was dozing off on the job. The Boy Jones was probably just as startled when he opened a door and their eyes met. Off ran the Boy Jones, scrambling into the darkness of the palace.

As the confusion and groggy shock faded, Cox reasoned it was his job to do something. So he finally chased after the boy, who was now long gone in the dim expanse of Buckingham Palace. The pursuit was fruitless until Cox tripped over a pile of random objects which should not have been sitting in the middle of a hallway.

It was probably a humorous sight to see him go tumbling over a mess of books, fabric, and other odds and ends, all of which were covered in dirty handprints. It wasn't funny to William Cox, though, especially after he found a sword in the pile of pilfered paraphernalia. The sword belonged to one of the queen's friends, who happened to have a room at the palace. Cox's stomach dropped; this meant the boy had been in someone's locked room.

When Cox arrived at the now-unlocked room, it was just as he expected. Everything was a mess, with the sooty grime of telltale handprints on nearly every surface, and the furniture in disarray. Unable to get a handle on the slippery situation by himself, he alerted more men to help scour the palace. Soon their worst fears were confirmed.

Given the circumstances, the men might have feared for their jobs as guards, but there were other, more important worries to deal with first. They soon discovered a letter with the very same grimy handprint on it. It was a letter to the queen. This meant the strange boy had been in the queen's own bedroom.

As funny as Cox's earlier tumble into a pile of dirty laundry might have been, the ensuing chase was probably even funnier. Like an old slapstick cartoon, the guards collided into each other at corners, scrambled in every direction, and literally lost their grip on the boy, thanks to his dirty, greasy clothing. Outwitted temporarily, they refused to let the boy get away. When they finally managed to pin him down, they were sure to keep a firm hold of the squirmy sneak. Out of breath and exasperated from the evening's comedy of errors, they marched him to one of the few well-lit rooms.

Finally able to get a good look at the boy, they searched his body from head to toe. Once panicked by the possibilities of the boy escaping with who-knows-what, the guards could now take solace in the fact that he wouldn't get out the door (which they should have locked) with any royal belongings. There was still one more surprise he had in store. Everyone, and I mean EVERYONE, was embarrassed to discover that, among the coins, trinkets, and keepsakes still in his pockets, the boy had several pieces of the queen's royal underwear.

The papers had a field day with tales of the Boy Jones. Amazingly, his intrusions weren't a one-time event. To the chagrin of palace staff, he snuck into the palace several times. It was strange enough that the Boy Jones seemed to appear within the walls of the palace, but the fact that he clearly knew his way around the massive building was even more alarming. His brazen acts and apparent comfort in the royal quarters exasperated officials, but to the general public, he was a welcome diversion from everyday life. People followed his cat-and-mouse game with palace guards with glee in the newspapers.

However, when the dirty boy was found sitting on the queen's throne, like the little brat owned the place, everyone decided he had gone too far. To pay for his intrusive crimes, the Boy Jones ultimately found himself aboard a prison ship bound for Australia, which is where British royalty sent their peskiest criminals.

Though he'd go down to Australia as punishment for his persistent pant-stealing peskiness, he'd also go down in history as the boy who stole Queen Vic's knickers. On top of that, how many people can say they sat their grubby butt on the same storied seat which had once supported the dignified derrières, baronial bottoms, and grandiose glutes of centuries' worth of British royal families?

Ironically, if the Boy Jones truly wanted to remember the queen with souvenir skivvies, he might have tried a more direct approach than breaking and entering. He could've tried being her friend.

Queen Victoria was such an important person that her name describes an entire 64-year era of western civilization. Her reign from 1837 to 1901 was longer than any British monarch's time on the throne before her, and everything from music and architecture to the scientific advancements that happened during her time are said to be products of the Victorian Era. Clothing was no different.

Victorian fashion brought major shifts in how women dressed. One major change was that their giant dresses no longer required dozens of petticoats or masses of hidden fabrics to fill out their bell shapes. These were replaced by simple steel and bone cages worn under a dress to create the same shape, only without all the shaping fabric underneath. While women found the old style of wearing lots of fabric under their dresses to be heavy, uncomfortable, and time-consuming to put on, they realized all those layers did keep a lady warm. Like many other women who followed the trend wearing of fewer layers of underwear, Victoria found that it got cold under there. Her solution was a different kind of underwear.

Victoria, queen of the largest empire in the world, she who lent her name to an entire era, had a passion for drawers. Today people calling their underwear *drawers* might not understand why the name exists, but for someone like Victoria it was very literal. Covering her royal heinie were two individual cloth leg coverings. These were attached to a drawstring, which was cinched, or drawn, around her waist (as you can imagine, nothing could be worse than a queen's underpants falling down). They kept her dresses clean, her skin comfortable, and her butt warm. She loved them so much that she ordered dozens of batches made on a near-constant basis. Some were silk and some were linen, but each  and every pair was embroidered with the royal insignia, a crown with the letters *VR*, which stood for her title in Latin, "Victoria Regina."

Perhaps she had heard the horrifying tale of King James I, who had rested his dirty-underweared bottom on the British throne many years before. He almost never took his underwear off and it is rumored that, at his death, doctors had to peel it from his body.

More likely, Victoria just enjoyed a really fresh pair. Whatever the reason was, she almost never wore the same underwear twice. Of course, her long life meant she went through a tremendous amount of undies. If you're the queen[6], then brand-new underwear is a daily option. The rest of us will most likely have to settle for an underwear collection numbering somewhere between Victoria and James I.

The question you may be asking yourself is, "What did Victoria do with all of those pairs of once-worn underwear?" One thing she did not do is toss them in the trash. It appears she saved many (there's a lot of storage in Buckingham Palace — apparently enough for 64 years' worth of underwear). The rest she gave away to her friends. It's not unusual to find a pair of her drawers in museum collections around the world. Heaven knows there should be plenty to go around. If he'd been patient, the Boy Jones might have even gotten a pair for himself.

---

[6] or American football quarterback Tom Brady, from what I hear

Queen Elizabeth I, Fashion-Forward Monarch

When a friend gave Elizabeth I of England a pair of silk stockings back in 1560, the queen loved them so much she immediately ordered more. Stockings themselves weren't new. Men and women had long worn cloth stockings woven from cotton and wool as both underwear and outerwear. However, once Elizabeth stuck her legs in stockings made from luxurious natural silk, a new trend began. Nobles practically bankrupted themselves trying to keep up with the Queen's newfound fashion passion. Elizabeth's silk-stocking craze stuck around for centuries after she was gone, but the fancy hosiery always remained expensive and fragile.

Centuries later, an alternative arrived at the 1939 World's Fair in New York City. Nylon was invented by the Dupont company as the first synthetic fiber. Rather than occurring naturally, it was made in great quantities by humans, and, on top of that, it was durable and cheap. The miracle material revolutionized stockings just as Elizabeth's silk had done centuries before. Though its first success was in legwear, today nylon is used for everything from carpets to ropes, tennis rackets, guitar strings, and even toothbrushes.

SHORT SHORT

Beau Brummell, Mr. Fancypants

For a period of time, Beau Brummell was the most fashionable man in England, which would have put him high in the running for the title of "Most Fashionable Man in the World," if there was such a thing. Today we might call him an "influencer," and his influence was enormous, despite the only social media of his day being gossip columns in newspapers.

In the early 1800s, he convinced people to throw away their ornate and fussy stockings, knee breeches, and flashy coats. Instead, he wore fitted trousers, clean linen shirts, and a fashionable cravat. It looked simple, but it was surprisingly difficult to achieve.

Some say he spent five hours a day bathing, shaving, tending to his clothes, dressing, and meticulously retying the cravat around his neck. His process was such a spectacle that it became a privilege for people to sit in his dressing room and watch him get dressed. Even his one-time friend King George IV would watch Beau hang out in his underwear as he painstakingly prepared his outfit for the day's events. His efforts and approach to dressing changed fashion in ways that we still see today, but luckily the trend of having everyone watch you get dressed never really caught on.

KEEP YOUR FRIENDS CLOSE, BUT KEEP YOUR UNDERWEAR CLOSER

Al Capone (1899–1947)

Things could've turned out differently for Alphonse Capone. Like many others in the 1800s, his parents left their homeland and crossed the ocean with a couple of kids and whatever they could fit in a trunk. They stepped onto Ellis Island in 1894 with wobbly sea legs, a handful of keepsakes, a few diapers for the boys, and a handful of clothes and underwear for themselves. Settling within eyesight of the Statue of Liberty, they quickly filled up their house with more children. Al was the fourth of nine, and because of the family's tight budget, he'd wear the hand-me-downs as soon as they got too tight for his three older brothers. There's no way to know how many of the Capone kids wore the same underwear, but for a big family in turn-of-the-century Brooklyn, underwear sharing was a way of life.

Despite having to feed a family the size of a baseball team, the Capones worked hard and carved out a decent life alongside the other immigrants in the neighborhood. Young Al was a smart kid and usually brought home good report cards, but things changed as he approached his teenage years. Whether it was the influence of bad boys in the neighborhood, or the simple dream of wearing his very own pair of fancy underwear (which he wouldn't have to share with anyone else), young Al Capone went down a dark path.

Sixth grade was the end of his formal schooling. He punched his teacher and walked out. As you might imagine, that's when things got off track. He fell in with a tough crowd, and a tough crowd in this time and place meant a life of crime. It started small with running petty errands for older gangsters. Then he moved on to some not-so-petty things like robberies. There was a whole bunch of fighting. This was how he wound up with the famous scar on his face. The guy who gave it to him might have done him a favor. As his legend grew, the papers would refer to him as "Scarface." Al didn't care for the name. Mobsters have feelings, too, and it hurt his when people used it. You've got to admit, though, it was an appropriately menacing nickname for someone who would become one of the most notorious criminals in history.

In his twenties, Al left the East Coast and moved to Chicago. It was an opportune time for a guy like him to be a gangster, and the Windy City was a perfect place for a criminal life. Most of the politicians and cops were just as corrupt as the criminals. If Al didn't want to get in trouble for something, all he had to do was pay off the authorities and they'd look the other way.

It was a pretty good arrangement for the people making money, but not for the general public. Citizens would have definitely preferred to have honest officials keeping them safe.

For years and years, many different groups in America had tried to make alcohol illegal across the country. They pointed to the crime and sickness it created, the productivity it lost, and the families it tore apart. After decades of effort, the teetotalers, as some called them, eventually won, and Congress ratified a law known as Prohibition in 1919. When the Eighteenth Amendment took effect in January of the next year, booze was illegal.

This didn't bother Al one bit. In fact, it would make him a very rich man. If anything, gangsters like Al knew that laws wouldn't stop people from wanting certain things. He made a career out of selling these things to people.

If he'd carried an accurate business card, it would've listed his occupations as "Election-meddling, Alcohol, Gambling, and more." Of course, he was too smart to put that in writing. One actual business card from his early years in Chicago said he sold used furniture and office supplies. But Al's furniture store was just a screen to hide all of the illegal stuff he did. If anyone was really paying attention, they surely would have noticed that the same few pieces of furniture were always on display in the same spots of the dingy showroom floor. For a store to stay in business, you have to sell something every now and again.

In truth, Al was selling something — it just wasn't chairs and desks. Really, he was part of an organized crime family which sold beer and liquor to speakeasies and other establishments. It was illegal, but you wouldn't have guessed it by walking around Chicago and its suburbs. People barely hid their alcohol, or anything else. If anyone started sniffing around and threatened to arrest or convict the booze-peddling offenders, the bribe of a fistful of dollars — or the threat of something more severe — usually took care of the problem before it went anywhere.

At first, Al's problems didn't come from the law; they came from other gangsters. Al and his team of thugs weren't alone. There were plenty of other gangs selling booze and, like dogs at a fence line, everyone was protective of their turf. During peaceful times, everyone tried to get along and stick to the agreed-upon boundaries. During the not-so-peaceful times, bullets went flying in every which way. New on the scene was the Thompson submachine gun. The tommy gun, as it was known,  was originally intended for the European war fronts of World War I, but when the war ended, the manufacturer made it available for sale to any would-be criminals with enough cash. If there's one thing a mobster has, it's cash.

TOMMY GUN

The new guns were able to spray an absurd amount of bullets, but they were very hard to handle, kicked like a sputtering mule, and rarely hit their target. They were accurate enough, though. Plenty of Al Capone's enemies met their end when the triggers were pulled. Whenever that happened, Al was nowhere to be found. Other people did his dirty work, which kept him out of the sight of witnesses. This is why he was always so hard to arrest. Never being at the scene made it next to impossible to connect him to the crime. Everyone knew he was in charge, but there was no way to prove anything. If a jury was ever going to send him to jail, the prosecutors would need proof that *he* committed a crime.

Al was no dummy. He made sure evidence was hard to come by. Financial records were destroyed or hidden in special safes that were almost impossible to open. Most important, he didn't keep any of his growing fortune in a bank. He was practically the King of Chicago, but on paper, he didn't have much to his name beyond a floundering furniture business. Al knew money in the bank was proof that he actually had that money. And if someone went looking into how he got all that money, it would start to be a big problem for him. So rather than create a paper trail, he spent it lavishly, and made a show of his bombastic lifestyle.

He hammed for the press so much the other mobsters got angry. Nearly anytime there was a crime thought to be his, he'd head down to the police station himself, saying "I heard you were looking for me." Capone always got off. Sometimes it was because the city official was already on his payroll; other times it was because there was none of that pesky evidence.

Rival gangsters tried to take justice into their own hands. Once his car was tailed by would-be assassins. Wildly inaccurate tommy

guns opened fire on the Capone vehicle, and when the smoke settled, they were surprised to learn that Al wasn't even inside. They were also surprised (and probably a little embarrassed) to learn that everyone who actually was inside survived the attack. Amazingly, the driver was not only safe, but he was unscathed. Whizzing bullets had pierced holes in his jacket and even his underwear, but his body was completely hole-free.

These public shootings started happening too often to ignore. Plus, the booze business was obviously out of control in its disregard of the Prohibition law. Perhaps even worse, Capone was making the national papers almost every day. Embarrassed that criminals had gotten so powerful, the federal government realized it had to get involved. While some Chicago police and politicians could be bought or silenced, Al would find out that the Feds were another matter altogether. He was branded Public Enemy Number One.

They knew he was a bad guy but, try as they might, they couldn't pin a crime on him. He was as slick as an oiled eel. Despite murders, booze, and hundreds of other crimes, Al Capone had covered his tracks so well that he still walked the streets, smiled for photos, and met with the press without an ounce of shame.

Then it clicked with the Feds: tax evasion. No matter how anyone makes money, citizens are required to pay taxes on their income. Since he had hidden all of his millions of dollars of dirty money, Al Capone hadn't paid a dime of taxes on it. Maybe it wasn't juicy like his other crimes, but this was their best bet to get him behind bars.

Their first challenge was proving that he actually had this money. Since he kept it out of the bank, it wasn't easy to trace. When they got a couple of his bookkeepers to flip on him, it opened some doors. Soon, they felt they could prove he was earning well over two million dollars a year, but knew he was actually making far more than that. Considering he hadn't paid taxes in a decade or more, they claimed he had willingly withheld a fortune from the United States government. Convincing a jury would be the second challenge.

Not long before the trial was set to begin, the judge got a tip. One of Al's henchmen had passed out wads of cash to everyone in the jury pool like cupcakes at a birthday party. Playing his cards better than Capone, the judge surprised everyone by switching jury pools with another judge just before the opening statements. Al's mouth dropped to the floor. The party was over.

The new jury settled in to hear how the government was going to prove Al Capone had lots of money when they couldn't prove it with bank statements. The answer was simple. Al Capone was well known for spending money like crazy. To see how lavish his spending truly was would prove he had a fortune hidden away — a fortune he had avoiding paying taxes on. On the contrary, every member of that jury had paid taxes, and they did so while wearing old underwear and the wrinkly suits.

A string of Capone's salesmen took the stand. From his suit dealer the jury heard how Al bought dozens of fancy suits and even paid extra to modify the right pocket in each one to hold his pistol. It's not a crime to have nice suits, Al's lawyers refuted. The jury, dressed in the same brown jackets they had probably worn to church that weekend, blinked their eyes.

Next the prosecution brought in his jeweler. Al liked diamonds so much that this guy had recently sold him eight diamond belt buckles for $275 each. It's not a crime to have nice jewelry, Capone's lawyers argued. In 1931, one of these belt buckles was worth about the same amount of money the average American worker earned in a year. The jury nodded.

Everything fell apart for Al Capone when a man named Mr. Oles came to the stand. Mr. Oles sold Al Capone underwear. Stifled laughter filled the otherwise stodgy courtroom when he began describing Capone's favorites. Capone himself couldn't help joining. It was hard to embarrass the man, but newspaper reporters caught him blushing during the description.

Mr. Oles testified that Al's favorite undies were an "athletic style underwear" and made from "glove silk." Most of the people in the room had never heard of glove silk, so the salesman enlightened the room. Glove silk is the same material used for the fanciest of lady's gloves. The laughter grew, at least until he told the court the price. Al's undies cost $12 a pair, which, in America during the Great Depression, was an entire week's wages for many. Capone was buying dozens of these fancy silk undershorts at a time.

No one was laughing anymore. Especially not the jury, sitting there in whatever uncomfortable, cheap undies they wore day in and day out.

It wouldn't take much more to find him guilty. Lawyers had proven that he had illegally earned a fortune and then refused to pay taxes on it. Bootlegging or murder didn't bring him down. His fancy underwear did.

He was sent to prison in Atlanta, but Al was not quick to give up the lifestyle or his comfy undies. The newspapers reported he was still calling the shots for  his empire of crime from behind bars and wearing $12 silk undies while he did it. He was also showing off for his new prison friends. To prove he could get anything in prison he could get in the outside world, he once paid for an ice cream truck to come and treat all of his fellow prisoners. This was all very embarrassing to the government, so they decided to send him to Alcatraz, a maximum security prison on an island off the coast of San Francisco, California. There was no way he could pull the same nonsense there.

It was true, he couldn't. But that didn't stop the press from spreading rumors of the same fancy underwear under the crime boss's clothes and same criminal commands coming from his jail cell. The warden shut down these rumors as fast as a getaway car on a Chicago freeway. Capone did not enjoy special treatment. Al wore the same itchy undies as everyone else. Actually, Capone was put on laundry duty, which meant he had to wash all the undies on the island. It was a long way down for the former King of Chicago.

SHORT SHORT

Vermin-proof Underwear

Life as a soldier during World War One was pretty miserable. American men on the war front spent a lot of time in muddy trenches, eating bland and unappetizing food, suffering long weeks of extreme weather, and praying that enemy bullets wouldn't leave an extra hole in their bodies. Though quite small, pests like lice were another huge problem. It's hard to imagine anything worse than dodging bullets in the mud while scratching the relentlessly itchy bites from the blood-sucking lice crawling around in your underwear, but this was the grim reality for many.

American women took it upon themselves to rid their soldiers of their parasitic pants pests. "Vermin-proof underwear" were created by Charlotte Eastman when she soaked underwear in a special chemical loathed by lice. The underpants quickly became a great deterrent to the annoying bugs. Women's groups raised funds to soak all the skivvies they could find in the solution and then sent them overseas by the thousands. American soldiers were fortunate that citizens back home realized that sometimes it's one's civic duty to protect someone else's booty.

GUGLIELMO MARCONI — UNDERWEAR OVERBOARD!

Guglielmo Marconi is remembered as the inventor of radio technology. His discoveries and creations changed the world by allowing people to communicate without wires for the first time in history. This all made him a very busy man.

While traveling on business across the Atlantic Ocean on a luxurious ocean liner in 1905, he was looking for ways to save himself some precious time. His wife grew confused one day when she walked into their room to find him standing suspiciously at the open porthole window. Mr. Marconi was throwing his socks and underwear out into the salty water of the Atlantic and she wanted to know why. He plainly explained it was easier to toss his used whites into the ocean and get new ones rather than to wait for the used ones to be laundered.

He may have been a visionary when it came to technology, but Marconi was very short-sighted when it came to keeping the oceans clean.

WHERE NO MAN HAS GONE BEFORE

Buzz Aldrin (1930–)

In the 1950s and 1960s, America and the Soviet Union were locked in a heated battle for interstellar dominance known as the Space Race. Scientists and astronauts (or cosmonauts, as they were known in Russia) worked around the clock to get a leg up on each other by getting anything and everything up into orbit. By the tail end of the 1960s, Neil Armstrong would make history with the ultimate accomplishment, but his full-bladdered buddy Buzz Aldrin made history in a very different way. Space-age undies helped carry these men to where no man had gone before. Once there, Buzz really *went* where no man had gone before, if you know what I mean.

Before Aldrin's universal urination, the Space Race was pretty lopsided — the Soviets were always getting their leg up higher and higher with a constant string of successes and firsts. In 1957, the Soviet Union launched Sputnik, the first satellite. They quickly followed the success of Sputnik by sending the first dog, Laika, to space. America was still struggling to get a satellite of their own into orbit by the time Russian cosmonaut Yuri Gagarin floated by from outer space.

Being the first human to gaze upon Earth from a perch in the cosmos was a clear win, and the cosmonaut certainly had a chance to stick out his tongue as he floated past the American continent on his single pass around the planet. If he had, it would have been another first — a fly-by mocking from space. There's no proof that Yuri's tongue-taunt actually happened, but if the race was a contest of each nation's outer space successes, it's safe to say America was getting whipped harder than butter in a churn.

President John Fitzgerald Kennedy wasn't ready to let the Soviet Union spread the United States space program on toast and eat it for breakfast. He made a bold prediction. America would skip right to the biggest, hardest, most seemingly impossible goal. They'd put a man on the moon before the 1960s drew to a close. Considering he made this giant leap of a claim in 1962, at a time when the Americans hadn't had a ton of success, the folks at NASA probably spit their morning coffee out over their toast. The president didn't really leave the brainiacs a lot of time.

To put it mildly, getting to the moon is a difficult task. There were rockets to build, vast calculations to compute, programs to write, astronauts to train, simulations to undergo, and underwear to design. Luckily, the goal was clear: walk on the moon. Everything else would just be details to work out along the way.

(Sad) Spoiler Alert: NASA would get people to the moon, but President Kennedy would not live to witness the interstellar success he had inspired. His assassination in 1963 left him six years short of seeing the dream come true. But even in his wildest dreams, he probably never imagined another first they'd accomplish. If he had, he might've rephrased his prediction from "We will put a man on the moon," to something like, "We will put a man on the moon, and he will be the first to pee there."

Buzz Aldrin was no stranger to flying (or peeing, for that matter). His dad flew planes during World War I and taught aviation for the United States Army. So when Buzz joined the air force in 1947, he was practically joining the family business. He stood out amongst his fellow students, soldiers, and pilots with his aerodynamic understanding and airborne abilities. He was also really smart, and great under pressure. These last two were excellent qualities for people to have when auditioning for the new job of astronaut. Also high on the list of ideal traits for would-be astronauts was being able to not puke their guts out while zooming around at 24,000 miles per hour. Buzz was perfect for the job.

For the record, Buzz was not his given name. His real name was Edwin. As the story goes, one of his younger siblings couldn't pronounce "brother" correctly, and instead referred to Edwin as "Buzzer." The family got so used to it that the name kinda stuck. Buzzer became Buzz, and Buzz became an astronaut.

Like the rest of America, he eagerly watched as NASA slowly made their way towards the moon. It was baby steps at first. With each of many different missions, new skills were gained and important new information was learned.

The first batch of missions was known as Project Mercury. The goal for these missions was to get American astronauts to space, orbit around Earth, and live to tell the tale. The Mercury program helped scientists envision the technology it would take to eventually get to the moon, as well as understand the effects space has on the human body.

At the next stage, known as Project Gemini, NASA learned and perfected intricate maneuvers and tasks while pushing the limits of their earthbound engineers and airborne astronauts. Gemini missions lasted longer to help understand how a body would react to remaining in space for weeks at a time. Then in 1965, the Gemini IV mission saw the first American leave a spacecraft to make a spacewalk. It was a huge moment. Of course, Russian cosmonauts beat them to it by floating in the great unknown a full two months before.

Undeterred by the string of second-place finishes, NASA kept their eyes on the moon prize. All the other missions had laid the groundwork for the Apollo program, which had the ultimate goal of landing, walking, and maybe even peeing on the surface of the moon. By the time they were ready for the moon mission with the now-historic Apollo 11 launch, Buzz Aldrin had earned a seat and was eager for his big moment. Three men would head to space for the mission, but only two would make it to the moon. It was determined that astronaut Michael Collins would need to remain in the main space shuttle. That meant Buzz would be in the Lunar Module, sharing the cramped space of the secondary vehicle with Neil Armstrong as it detached from the main shuttle and landed on the moon's surface.

Every single detail of the mission had to be perfect. NASA doesn't like surprises. A surprise in space means a dead person in space, and a dead person in space means a mummy in space. There's no oxygen out there, which is what a body needs to decompose. With no oxygen or gravity, well, that's how you get floating space mummies.  Buzz and Neil were hoping to stay very much alive and non-mummified. One huge detail in the no-mummy moon master plan was what they would wear.

You can't survive space in your jeans. Bad stuff would happen, which is why astronauts wear space suits instead. Astronauts enclose themselves in these uncomfortable, shell-like outfits to create a safe atmosphere for their bodies. The suits are pressurized, rigid, and fed with oxygen to breathe. After one of the previous Apollo missions caught fire and killed the three men on board, NASA had to take their clothing material choices very seriously. Scientific advancements didn't just extend to rockets and radars. In the 1960s, there were all sorts of new man-made fabrics that would give future fliers a fair shot by being fire-resistant.

But sometimes safety and comfort don't mix. Especially when it comes to underwear. Amazing new space-age fabrics were used for nearly everything, but the spacemen got grumpy when they found the new materials pressed against their sensitive space-bottoms. Nothing at the time felt as good and allowed a body to breathe and perspire as well as good old-fashioned (but flammable) cotton. So despite it being a potential fire hazard, Buzz and the guys wore cotton underwear. They wore their cotton undies all the time. In fact, they wore them so often that the underwear coveralls were officially called the CWG, or Constant Wear Garment.

It took the men 76 hours to make the 240,000-mile journey to the moon. While they sped their way to their lunar destination, the three men didn't have much to do other than hang out in the same underwear they had first shimmied into back on launch day. There was no way to freshen up the wardrobe. Ease of motion was not the biggest consideration when it came to designing the first moon-bound spacecraft. Even if a costume change had been easy, the men had few options. Every ounce of weight mattered, so they didn't bring much else to wear. Obviously there was no washing machine aboard, either. To say the least, the Apollo astronauts had to get very, very comfortable with each other and their CWGs.

When Neil and Buzz left their pal Michael Collins in the space shuttle to land the even more cramped and less cozy Lunar Module on the moon surface, they would finally be able to switch out their three-day-old undies for a more technologically advanced underwear. Meanwhile, through another incredible leap of science, millions of TVs back on Earth tuned in for the once-in-a-lifetime broadcast of the big event. When the Lunar Module landed, the twosome inside had a choice: take a nap (they hadn't slept much in the last 24 hours), or go for a moonwalk. Knowing Americans were awake and gathered around their televisions, Buzz and Neil opted to make history in prime time.

While Americans were watching back on Earth and waiting for the dramatic moment to unfold, there was a painfully slow, choreographed dance of dress-up going on that no one could see. Hidden inside the lunar lander, the men spent an anticlimactic three hours getting dressed in their special gear and revolutionary moon suits.

Despite the cramped quarters, the pair was comfortable enough with each other to finally take off their CWGs and change into a different kind of underwear — liquid-cooled long johns. These weren't too different from long underwear we wear down on Earth, but these space versions had some additions to keep their body temperature low while they were work-  ing in heavy suits and an extreme envi- ronment. Small tubes were sewn into the fabric, connecting key points all over the body. Inside these tubes, water was constantly cycled around the underwear. The water worked as a conductor to help keep body temperatures cool by absorb- ing body heat. As the water passed through a special device in the suit, it was re-cooled before heading back out through the tubes to do it all again.

This wasn't the only kind of tube in the suit, though. There was also a pee tube. Stop and think about it for a second. Whatever your mind conjures up is probably pretty close to the actual thing. It was a practical solu- tion to a real problem: *Where does the pee go when nature calls?* Thanks to this device, when an astronaut let loose, the pee would travel through the tube to a collection bag. The bag could be removed and simply left in space. Just as before, every ounce of weight was going to count for the return journey. Besides, no one wanted it back on Earth.

It was a great design, but unfortunately Buzz encoun- tered a problem. The landing of the Lunar Module had gone smoothly, but there were unforeseen complications with the ladder they lowered to the desolate moonscape. Earthbound viewers might not have noticed, but on his descent Neil was surprised to discover that the last rung of the ladder was still three feet from the lunar surface. This was unexpected, but it didn't stop him. After a brief pause he jumped down and soon spoke his famous words about small steps and giant leaps. Those first moments on the moon were an incredible culmination of decades of work, sacrifice, and science. President Kennedy would have been proud.

Not far behind, Buzz made his way down the ladder to make a little history of his own. Neil warned him that the last step was a doozy but Buzz still stretched a bit too far as he put his foot down, eager to become only the second moonwalker. The stretch resulted in a small tear. Fortunately the tear was inside the space suit, and not out (that's how you get floating space mummies). Unfortunately, it was the Urine Collection Device that Buzz had torn.

Buzz had a lot on his mind when nature inevitably came calling. He probably didn't even think about those millions of eyes watching when he let loose. It's not as if they could have known, anyway. That big suit did offer plenty of privacy. So with the world watching he secretly peed the first pee on the moon. And that pee never made it to his torn Urine Collection Device. Instead, it wound up floating inside the leg of his space suit.

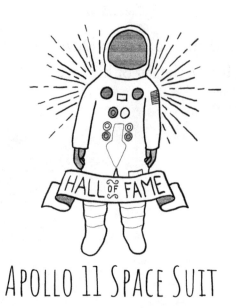

Apollo 11 Space Suit

Sure, the space suit is not *exactly* underwear, but had it not been for some dedicated *underwear makers*, Buzz Aldrin and Neil Armstrong might not have survived their trip to the moon in their special suits.

Temperatures are extreme on the moon, but scorching highs and far-below-freezing lows were just one concern. With no ozone layer, solar radiation left lunar travelers looking for a suit to keep them safe from several things. On top of that, the suit had to ward off the thousands of micrometeoroids constantly whirring around the moon's surface faster than speeding bullets. If one of those pee-wee projectiles put even the tiniest of holes in a space suit, the astronaut inside would quickly become an astro-NOT.

Military contractors, engineering firms, and smart minds of all kinds tried to figure out how to make a suit that would not only keep the person inside safe, but give them mobility and flexibility to do the work the mission required. No one could figure it out until someone from a Delaware-based company called Playtex convinced NASA to give them a shot at solving the problem.

The Playtex Company was founded when a Ukrainian immigrant named Abram Spanel began selling rubber diaper covers door-to-door. Unfortunately Buzz Aldrin didn't have one of those for his moon walk, but luckily the company would support him in other ways. Playtex expanded, and by the 1960s, their main business was making women's underwear such as girdles and bras. Employing many of the same materials they used for their underwear line, and the same steady, skilled hands of Playtex seamstresses, the company knew they could deliver a safe, sturdy, and flexible space suit.

After helping engineers understand what was possible to do with the fabric, and collaborating on design, Playtex's team of women hand-stitched the suits to perfection. Like much of the world, the underwear makers watched nervously as Neil Armstrong and Buzz Aldrin finally fulfilled the dream of walking on the moon. The safety and the success of the mission rested on many people, but perhaps none more so than the skillful seamstresses at Playtex.

By the Seat of His Pants
Buster Keaton (1895–1966)

Buster Keaton went to school only one day in his life. His dad figured some time in the classroom might be good for the boy, so one day he woke the boy up early, got him dressed, and sent him on his way. At the end of the day, the youngster came home with a note from the teacher asking that he not return. Buster cared more about making his classmates laugh than following his teacher's directions. He was sent home for being too funny. If only there had been a fire drill that day, perhaps she could've seen his true value (not to mention his underpants).

Plenty of people can say they had an unusual childhood. However, not very many can say they were thrown across a stage every night, that they got their nickname from Harry Houdini, or that this name came as a result of a terrifying childhood accident. Buster could say all of this, and though his name at birth was Joseph, he would almost never hear anyone use it.

His parents were vaudeville performers, which was popular entertainment before the days of TVs, radios, and smartphones. Vaudeville shows included acts of music, comedy, magic, drama, and more, all staged for a live theatre audience. When little Joseph was too young for underwear and was making messes in diapers instead, he was packed along as his parents performed with a vaudeville group that included legendary escape artist Harry Houdini.

Even as a toddler, Joseph Keaton was a rambunctious and fearless little fellow. One day he scurried off and found himself staring down a long flight of stairs without batting either of his big brown baby eyes. His parents were not close enough to react, or didn't really care about the long fall that awaited the child. Either way, they weren't winning any Parent of the Year awards.

There is a right way to use steps, and a bunch of wrong ways to use steps. On this day, little Joseph Keaton demonstrated one of the wrong ways. One by one, top over toes, the poor little guy thumped and thudded his way down every step. To anyone watching, the tumbling toddler probably seemed to move in horrifying slow motion. When he finally came to rest mercifully at the bottom, the boy sat up, looked a little dazed for a moment, and then shook himself back to normal. No tears, no pain, and no problem. The adults nearby breathed a sigh of relief. Years later, Keaton said it was Harry Houdini himself who scooped up the fallen boy off the ground and exclaimed, "That was a real buster!"

It became both a nickname and a way of life. Buster just seemed to have a knack for falling and not getting hurt. As soon as he could walk, he was onstage with his parents, and the comedy act became a family affair. Sure, having him onstage was a way to keep the little squirt out of trouble, but the Keatons also made use of the three-year-old's natural abilities. Part of the act required him to disobey his father onstage. Luckily this came naturally to him, as it does for most kids his age. The other part of the act required him to be picked up and thrown through the air.

Nothing like this would be allowed to happen today (and it certainly shouldn't!), but every night when the curtain went up, Buster's dad would heave him across the stage, hurl him out a fake window, even chuck him into the audience! With a limber body and a straight face (because no one likes it when you laugh at your own jokes — just kidding, I laugh at mine all the time), the kid just got right back up, time and time again. The audience didn't know what to make of it at first. It's certainly

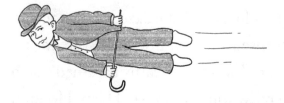

shocking to see a little kid go sailing across the room, but when he gets back up and asks for more, well, that could be pretty entertaining.

Anytime someone inquired with concern about Buster's well-being, he could show that his falls left him with no bumps, bruises, or broken bones. He was a natural tumbler. Eventually, though, he got a little too heavy for his dad to toss with ease. The smaller the kid, the easier it is to get a good throwing grip. Once a kid gets to be around school age, it's really hard to keep the proper form needed to launch him into a crowd full of people.

They say necessity is the mother of invention, but one could also call it the father of forward motion. Mr. Keaton devised a solution to the whole "tossing your growing kid" dilemma, and it was what Buster wore underneath his stage suit. Peeking out of a hidden incision in his fancy clothes were a pair of old suitcase handles attached to a stout fabric worn underneath the outfit. Now, with ease, Papa Keaton could grab these suckers and seriously send his son sailing.

Buster flew across vaudeville stages for as long as he reasonably could, but eventually he got far too heavy for his old man to toss, even with the underwear handles. It was for the best, because by the time Buster was a young man, silent films had taken the world by storm.

Vaudeville was quickly replaced by motion pictures on the silver screen as the most popular entertainment, even though the movies didn't have any sound. A childhood career of making people laugh with his straight face and perfect pratfalls put him in a great position for the new art form. The seemingly indestructible young man was tailor-made for moving pictures, and before long he was one of the biggest stars. It wasn't just because people couldn't believe the stunts he pulled; he was also hilariously funny and could tell a story without saying a single word. In a movie, more people than ever could watch him risk his neck and then wonder how he never got hurt.

Grabbing ahold of a passing car to make a hasty getaway is a terrible idea, but Buster did it. Falling down a flight of stairs is a terrible idea, but Buster did it over and over again (these times it was on purpose). Running inside of a steamboat's moving paddle wheel like a giant hamster is also a terrible idea, but Buster did that, too. Theatre audiences gasped and laughed, just as he had hoped fellow classmates would have done during his only day at school all those years before.

Sometimes his stunts were so dangerous that the camera crew couldn't bear to watch. When he arranged for the entire front of a house to fall on him, they simply turned the camera on and walked away. They expected him to be flattened like a pancake, but he was confident in his calculations. As the dust settled after the incredible collapse, there stood Buster, standing safely  in the space of an open window without even a scratch. The falling facade became one of his most famous feats.

With acts like this, Buster proved to be so good that he earned more and more control of his movies. He wasn't just a stone-faced star and super stuntman; the little kid who used to get thrown around by his underwear also became his own writer and director, and in 1926 he decided to make his masterpiece. If you think the American Civil War is a strange subject for a silent comedy, you're not alone. Most of the theatre audiences did, too. *The General* was not very popular when it was released, but today it is not just considered one of Buster's greatest achievements but also one of the most important movies ever made.

The General also featured the most expensive scene ever shot for a film up to that time. For a cost of $40,000 (over a half-million dollars, today), Buster engineered an explosive train crash that brought a giant locomotive from the top of a high wooden bridge to the bottom of a river in a matter of seconds. Special effects were very basic at the time and CGI was almost a century away, so this ambitious scene had to happen in real life. Of course, you can only destroy a bridge and real locomotive train once, so they'd 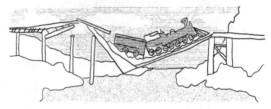 only have one shot to get the moment on film. Knowing there was going to be a once-in-a-lifetime spectacle, 4,000 eager spectators came to take their only chance at seeing such a crazy sight.

For obvious reasons, the train would need to be empty when it chugged onto the bridge, but Buster was a stickler for detail. Inside, the crew placed several dummies with papier-mâché heads to give the appearance of soldiers on board. No one thought to tell the spectators on the banks about the fake bodies, so when the train chugged into view, there was growing concern for the men they thought were still on board. Then the bridge collapsed in a fantastic display of fire and smoke. The lumbering locomotive tumbled and plunged into the river, like a baby Buster heaved into a pool by his father.

At this point, excitement gave way to panic for a few in the crowd. As one of the fake heads came floating down the river with no body in sight, a woman screamed in mistaken fear until she passed out. Had she or any of the other onlookers stuck around for a few more days, they would've had a very real reason to panic.

For the movie's climactic battle scene, Buster hired 500 Oregon National Guard members to play soldiers in the heated contest. Men would run one direction in Union Blue uniforms, quickly strip down to their undershirts and drawers, put on Confederate Gray uniforms, and run the other direction as opposing soldiers. Adding to the realistic chaos of a battle, cannons and rifles were fired in all directions.

The weapons weren't loaded, but each one was still igniting with very real sparks and flames. Sparks and flames are a terrible match for the dry brush and grass of the Oregon countryside, which is exactly where they were shooting the scene. And a brush fire is exactly what happened.

Buster was the kind of guy who came prepared with hoses, tanks of water, and a ready crew. Fire didn't come as a total surprise to him, but the speed and intensity of the blaze that popped up sure did. In about the same amount of time it took a diapered baby Buster to fall down a flight of stairs, fire spread in all directions. Flames surrounded the extras, the crew, and the movie star himself, quickly devouring whatever was in the path.

Five hundred National Guardsmen who had doubled as Union soldiers and tripled as Confederates now had to quadruple as firemen. Without hesitation, the men sprung into action, only to realize that while they had enough people to fight, they were short on water. In order to save the countryside, as well as the nearby town in the fire's path, they would need a water-free way to extinguish the fire. With flames dancing around his legs and smoke stinging his eyes, Buster did what anyone else in this book would have done. He took off his pants.

Fighting a fire is brave. Fighting it in your underwear with your dramatically divested trousers is another thing entirely. Ignoring the singed leg hair and shin burns on his now-bare skin, Buster frantically slammed his pants into the fire surrounding him. He beat it down until all that remained was a smoking spot of charred soot. Inspired by the movie star, the others on set followed his lead. Hundreds of hastily removed pants began smacking the ground in a field full of smoke and men in dirty white drawers. The passioned, pantless performance worked. As they beat the fire into submission,

others were able to use the remaining water to finish the job.

Standing in his skivvies, surveying the aftermath, Buster took pride in his quick thinking. His selfless actions had inspired others to shed their slacks when duty called. A few weeks later they took a less stressful break from filming when the National Guard held a ceremony to make him an honorary captain, both for his display of bravery and underwear. Mostly the bravery.

Buster continued making movies after *The General* despite the initial lukewarm reaction to the movie. Nothing else he made was quite as ambitious (or revealing). When "talkies" (which was a nickname for the first movies with sound) made it to theaters at the end of the 1920s, his career began to slow down. Maybe his brand of humor wasn't made for movies with sound, or maybe his body just couldn't take any more of the demanding stunt work that made him famous. Either way, Buster Keaton has gone down in history as one of the most important physical comedians, directors, and movie stars of his era. He will always be remembered as someone who put his body on the line to get the job done. Whether that meant flying across the stage, letting a house fall on him, or fighting a fire in his boxers, he was always eager to do what no one else could. And if it made people laugh, all the better.

SHORT SHORT

Ludwig von Beethoven — Naked Practice Makes Perfect

Composer Ludwig von Beethoven was more comfortable at his piano than anywhere else. Nothing stood between him and time spent tickling the ivories — not even his clothes! He famously persevered at his piano when he lost his hearing (a terrible fate for a musician, to be certain), but he also practiced with unshakeable dedication through regular bouts of chronic diarrhea.

When he wasn't suffering gastrointestinal trauma, friends would occasionally visit, only to be ignored as Beethoven sat at his piano, completely absorbed in a new piece of music. Typically, he'd be perched at the piano in nothing but his underwear, which seemed to be his preferred attire for writing. Other times, much to the embarrassment of his poor friends, the composer didn't bother wearing anything at all. It's likely that one of the greatest composers of all time may have written some of his most memorable melodies in the total absence of clothes.

Jelly Roll Morton – Hiding Diamonds

Jelly Roll Morton liked to tell people that he invented jazz music. To be fair to the many other adventurous musicians of the time, it was more of a group effort. Lofty claims aside, Jelly Roll was very important to the early development of the musical style. He was an incredible pianist, an innovative bandleader, and a great songwriter. He was also an avid gambler.

Most gamblers have ups and downs. Sometimes you're broke and sometimes you're flush with cash. On the rare occasions when his wallet was full from a string of wins, Jelly Roll loved to spend his earnings on diamonds. To keep these diamonds safe he'd pin them to his underwear. Once, he enjoyed an entire summer-long vacation with the gemstones hidden beneath his clothes. He figured this was the safest place to keep them away from the eyes of any potential thieves, and if you consider the endless sweaty days in the hot summer sun, he was probably right.

Eponymous Underpants
Amelia Bloomer (1818–1894)

In the 1800s, wearing a dress could be a real drag. I mean that literally. Some of those gargantuan gowns were so gigantic that they often grazed the ground beneath the feet of any woman wearing one. You could argue that the big, bell-shaped dresses were more than just a fashion statement, though. In a way, women's fashion became a form of substitute street cleaning. Trash collection was a thing of the future, and in a lot of places, people didn't pick up after themselves. If they did, it meant they threw whatever they didn't want in their house out of their house onto the streets below.

An afternoon stroll could quickly turn into an awful mess for any dignified ladies walking down those squalid and soiled streets in a fancy dress. Fine fabrics of every color could eventually wind up with a hemline of grimy brown as the costumes gathered garbage, dangled in the mud, and even dragged through the droppings horses left behind in the streets. Even if a lady managed to keep her dress clean, it would still be wildly cumbersome.

In the late nineteenth century (which is the confusing way to say "the 1800s"), many women were fed up with the way society expected them to live their lives. Yes, the size and lack of comfort of their clothes was frustrating, but an enormous dress made it hard to do anything much more than stand around, and even that was difficult. 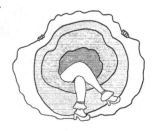 Ladies were also longing for freedom to roam and explore beyond the walls of their homes. Many young women were not permitted to drag their dress anywhere without a chaperone.

Those matters paled in comparison to the biggest goal they were working towards: suffrage. More women than ever were demanding a role in politics and it soon became an organized fight for the right to vote. Clothing had more to do with it than you might think.

Amelia Bloomer was one of these suffragists (which is a fancy word for someone who worked to get women the right to vote). She also had strong opinions about fashion, and as a result, her name is an eponym for a kind of underwear today. To be clear, Amelia didn't invent bloomers, she just knew a good idea when she saw one. It was another uncomfortably clad lady named Elizabeth Smith Miller who made them a reality.

Like many of her generation, Elizabeth had spent years in a garbage-grabbing dress that seemed as big as a church bell and nearly as heavy. People told the unsatisfied upstart designer that the constricting clothes she had been wearing were no big deal. A woman's work at the time was much less demanding than a man's! What need would she have for a silly indulgence like mere comfort? She probably got  as tired of hearing this nonsense as she did wearing the actual dresses.

Luckily, Elizabeth was a vestment visionary who decided she had had enough. Some might have called her crazy, but she pictured a world where women could enjoy the simple pleasure of sitting down without eclipsing behind an upturned hoopskirt. She dreamed of easily bending over to grab something on the floor, and she saw a future of walking through a room without leaving a trail of upturned furniture on the ground like spent bowling pins. Perhaps most of all she just wanted to breathe. But these were all things her clothes didn't really allow. So she scrapped the suffocating corset and birdcage-like structure under her skirt, tossed the mess of fabric into the closet, and set to work with scissors and thread, inspired by the memory of something she had seen on a trip across the ocean.

She finished one fateful day in 1851 and stepped out her door and into the free air, wearing — brace yourself, kids — billowy white leg coverings that reached her ankles. Covering these long underwear-like leggings was a skirt that broke well below her knees. Elizabeth said "no" to the dress!

At the time, the outfit was most often referred to as pantalettes (the leg-covering underclothes), and tunic (the skirt which made it so easy for her to move her legs). Imagine people's shock when she crossed the yard and not a single twig got stuck in her new outfit! Elizabeth didn't even knock over any tables in her living room! How undignified! Perhaps most shocking of all: it didn't take her an hour or more to cinch her corset breathtakingly tight, and install all of the necessary parts that would provide the poof underneath. What on earth would she do with all of the time she saved by wearing something so simple? Something devilish, no doubt.

The criticisms rolled off Elizabeth like water off a beaver-fur swimsuit, because she had the courage to wear a skirt with sensible pantaloons as underwear. If there had been cars, they would've wrecked as she strolled by. If there had been cameras, the paparazzi would've tumbled over one another for the perfect scandalous photo. On the whole, the 1850s were pretty free from these modern inventions, though, and the only thing there was to spread the shocking word of her costume was, well, the written word.

Some people loved the outfit, but plenty of people simply couldn't handle it. Those detractors made sure to get a lot of ink in the newspapers, talking about what an abomination the clothing combo was. If history can confirm anything, it's that haters have always hated.

Amelia Bloomer was someone who would fall head over heels for the outfit that broke just above her ankles. In 1849, Amelia had helped found a newspaper called *The Lily*. The women who started it planned for it to be "devoted to the interests of women." Unfortunately, the other ladies weren't as devoted as Amelia, and they soon left her high and dry, alone, to do the job. Since it was early in the paper's life, not many would have noticed had she just canned the whole project. Amelia resolved not to walk away and let people think that women couldn't follow

through on a such a lofty idea. So she became the editor, publisher, and regular writer.

The Lily mostly printed articles about what its founding women agreed to be the two most important issues: suffrage and temperance. People of the temperance movement wanted to convince Americans to stop drinking alcohol. Bloomer's newspaper did this by regularly publishing stories of drunk men meeting their doom in terribly  stupid ways, like falling into vats of boiling oil. Sharing gory details of foolish deaths was a striking way to illustrate the dangers drunkenness posed to a family.

Between the articles about drunk dudes high-diving into boiling hot cauldrons of dumb, *The Lily* published articles and editorials in favor of universal suffrage and women's rights. Amelia made the argument that not a single woman in America had any say in the many laws that affected them. This was completely unfair. Women couldn't vote, they couldn't hold office, and they really didn't even have much control of their own lives.

For its first few years, Amelia published the paper to a modest audience of around 400 subscribers, but it just takes one post to go viral. When the paper got involved in changing the way women dressed, Amelia went viral (or at least the nineteenth-century version of viral).

It began with a visit from her friend and fellow suffragist Elizabeth Cady Stanton. Stanton had recently seen Elizabeth Miller's fashion-forward pantalettes and tunic combo and immediately ditched her dresses in favor of the new outfit. Eager to share the joys of the versatile and free-moving clothing, she paid a visit to her pal.

Amelia knew a good thing when she saw it. She was smitten and she knew others would be, too. *The Lily* would be a great way to spread the word. On the pages of the paper, Amelia gushed about the many freedoms the clothing would give women, both inside the home and out. She included detailed descriptions of both the pantalettes underneath and the tunic that was worn over top.

For those excited by the new fashion and wishing to try some out for themselves, she printed instructions for making your own set. At the time, people couldn't head to the store and easily purchase fitted clothing, especially brand new, societal-norm-shattering clothing. Most people who couldn't hire someone to make their clothes for them took a Do-It-Yourself approach. It was not unusual for folks to sew both their own outerwear and underwear.

Bolstered by people's rabid interest in the radical new clothing, the paper's subscriptions ballooned to nearly 4,000 names. Not long after, ladies in the daring new outfit were strolling cleanly through the dirty streets of towns all over the country, scaring the establishment with the threat of easy movements, poop-free hemlines, and healthy, un-squished internal organs.

One big question still lingered on everyone's minds, though: "What do we call this outfit?" Though somewhat descriptive, Pantalette and Tunic Combo had the same amount of zing as a rusty can of nails. Because so many people learned about it through her newspaper, the outrageous ensemble began to be called the Bloomer Costume, and eventually "bloomers" became the name for the long pants worn underneath the skirt.

For several years, the Bloomer Costume was a ferocious fashion trend, empowering women all over the country, but eventually, Amelia herself gave up on the garments. She was tired of the controversy they created. People just wanted to talk about clothes, rather than the real issues: women's rights. In retrospect, the Bloomer Costume may have been a little ahead of its time. But sometimes it takes a jolt like this to change the way society thinks. A few decades later there was a Bloomer resurgence.

In the 1890s a new fad dominated America: bicycles. Everyone wanted to be riding bikes, and it got much easier to do so. Those huge-wheeled monstrosities known as "penny-farthings" fell out of favor, probably because they were difficult to even mount. Instead, there was a new kind of bike, called the safety bicycle. These closely resembled the bike you might ride around the neighborhood today. Women, weary of being stuck at home, excitedly adopted this new bike as their own. It was so common to see women riding these two-wheelers that they also became known as "ladies' bikes."

But it was dangerous at first. Yet again, big, billowy dresses caused a problem. It was a new, unforeseen problem Amelia never would've imagined, though. It was easy for any of that fabric flying around to get stuck in the sprockets, chains, or spinning tires of the bike. One unlucky move and the rider could be grated like cheese or sent flying to the ground below in torn rags that used to be a dress.

The solution was simple. The Bloomer Costume, with its separate, leg-covering underwear and skirt, allowed a rider to straddle the seat and conquer the world. It might sound silly, but in a way it's true. The bicycle, which women rode with ease, thanks to their more manageable under and outerwear, introduced many to independence and autonomy. This would eventually help lead to the ultimate goal of women's suffrage.

When the Nineteenth Amendment was passed in 1920, after decades of struggle, many American women got to vote for the first time in history. Many still, like Black women and Native Americans, would have to wait longer. But the Constitutional  Amendment of 1920 marked an important moment in the march for equality. Susan B. Anthony, perhaps the most famous suffragist in America, said it had a lot to do with bicycles.

"Let me tell you what I think of bicycles," she said. "I think it has done more to emancipate women than anything else in the world. It gives women a feeling of freedom and self-reliance. I stand and rejoice every time I see a woman ride by on a wheel. It gives her a feeling of self-reliance and independence the moment she takes her seat: and away she goes, the picture of free, untrammeled womanhood."

The bicycle was the symbol of self-reliance, resistance, and even adventure for women of the time. And it wouldn't have been possible without bloomers.

ELLA GIFFT — SUFFRAGE SURPRISE

Not all suffragists were part of the temperance movement. In the U.S. Virgin Islands, Ella Gifft made money during Prohibition by selling illegal alcohol that she would sneak into the Caribbean hidden in her pantalettes. That wasn't all she hid in her underwear, though.

She was an active suffragist who helped found the Suffragist League on the islands, and when United States President Herbert Hoover came for a visit to St. Thomas, she arranged to meet him. When she began to pull something from under her clothes in front of the President, guards were worried it might be an assassination attempt. All were relieved to learn she was not armed with a gun, but rather a legal petition requesting that the Virgin Islands, a United States territory, be allowed to elect their own governor. It worked, and in 1931 the first civilian governor was elected in the Virgin Islands. By 1936, women were allowed to vote in those elections.

A Particular Pompadour Purple

Today there are dyes for every color you can imagine, but once upon a time, color options were pretty limited. Dyes came from natural sources and people were eager to find new colors for clothes in order to express their individuality.

The 56th Regiment of Foot was a British infantry regiment famous for wearing a very particular shade of purple. But they weren't the only ones. It was said that a famous French woman named Madame de Pompadour preferred her underwear to be the very same hue. Since their purple uniforms matched her favorite shade for undies, the military regiment became known as the "Pompadours."

From Burlap to Silk
Satchel Paige (1906–1982)

Some people earn their first paycheck scooping ice cream or sweeping floors. Leroy Paige earned his first dime carrying underwear around the train station in Mobile, Alabama. His mother had sent him there to earn some extra money for the family. For 10 cents Leroy would sling bags, suitcases, and satchels over his shoulder and carry them to departing trains for tired travelers. He wasn't alone. There were several other kids there competing for the same few dimes. Lanky Leroy had an advantage in size, and he knew how to hustle, so he usually managed to carry a few more bags than the others.

Ten cents might have been more valuable in 1920 than it is today, but Leroy wasn't exactly bringing home the bacon. Other family members were working too, but the huge family needed him to earn more. The truth was obvious: a lanky kid can carry only so many bags, even with 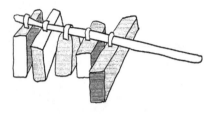 a strong body and a helpful hustle. Like a train arriving at the station, the solution to his problem popped into his head. Luckily that's not where it hit him, because the solution was a big, heavy stick.

Paige claimed his new stick-based solution was actually how he earned the nickname he'd answer to for the rest of his life. While other boys were hauling just one or two bags from here to there, Leroy would be tying as many as a dozen bags to his big stick. By slinging it over his shoulder and balancing it as he walked, he was able to carry four times as many bags as before. This put four times as many dimes in his pocket.

To everyone at the station, this solution was a funny sight to see. As the long, lumbering, bag-dangling branch weaved through the hallways, one startled person exclaimed that he looked like a walking satchel tree. Soon, Satchel became his name.

Satchel's big family was about as poor as poor gets. Everything — even underwear — had to be shared. Constantly the Paiges were trying to cut corners and save money. This meant they moved a lot. Each time it was the same. They'd squeeze almost a dozen family members into another tiny rental shack, like a sack bulging with too many potatoes. This was probably another reason he spent so much time at the station — there was no room at home! As helpful as he was to his family, he did give his mom some heartburn and sleepless nights with his poor behavior.

Another story says Satchel's name didn't come from his moneymaking satchel stick at all, but instead because he got caught red-handed sneaking off with someone else's satchel. The story of Satchel stealing satchels seems reasonable, though, because not long after working the train station for spare change, he wound up working involuntarily at the Alabama Reform School. It broke his mom's heart, because it was basically a jail for young boys — or so they both thought when they heard the judge's orders.

As it would turn out, it was a home inspired by a famous man named Booker T. Washington. He believed in reform through hard work and learning skills, which would very much be the case with young Satchel.

As he grew into a young man, Satchel would become a very different person than the one who first walked through those doors. He went to class (something he had never done before), milked cows, tended a garden, and turned heads singing lead in the choir. He also met a baseball coach who changed his life.

Baseball was something he had casually played with friends between chores and the train station, but he had never thought he could take it seriously. The coach realized this long, lanky kid had a body made for pitching.

This wasn't exactly surprising to Satchel. He could whip an oyster shell like cannon shot and take the bark off of a tree from 30 paces. Rumors spread (probably by Satchel) that he could knock a bird right out of the sky with a rock. There's probably 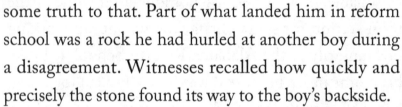 some truth to that. Part of what landed him in reform school was a rock he had hurled at another boy during a disagreement. Witnesses recalled how quickly and precisely the stone found its way to the boy's backside.

Thanks to encouragement from the coach, Satchel spent any free moment throwing a baseball. One pitch was all he had: a fastball. But it was superfast, so it was all he really needed.

Four years later, he returned home to a mother who was truly impressed with how her son had grown. Then she made it clear that, while it was great to see him and all, the family was still dirt poor. Almost immediately she sent him out to earn money. A regular job didn't sound like much fun to him, and he definitely wasn't going back to the station to haul people's undies.

Throughout the south there were amateur baseball teams looking for good players. Satchel went for a tryout. As soon as they saw him throw his fastball, he was hired. Playing baseball was a fun job for Satchel. Unfortunately, these amateur baseball teams just didn't pay enough to live on. A dollar a day was hardly enough to feed himself, let alone his family members. He set his sights on the professional sports league for Black players, known at the time as the Negro League.

At this time in America, there was a completely unfair and racist rule that Black players could not play on a Major League Baseball team. While players like Ty Cobb and Babe Ruth were on the sports page daily, there were hundreds of Black players who were just as good — or better — playing incredible baseball every day. Hardly anyone would ever learn their names, because the Negro Leagues were not covered by most newspapers or radio. At least not until Satchel Paige came along.

Satchel was nearly empty-handed in 1926 when he showed up to join one of the Negro League's more promising teams in Chattanooga. All he carried was a brown paper bag stuffed with a few meager possessions: two pairs of socks, one spare pair of dusty, hand-me-down pants, and — wrapped up and hidden in the pants — an extra pair of plain, old, worn-out underwear.

Looking around at his established and well-dressed teammates, it ate him up that he was still wearing old, worn-out clothes. That first paycheck couldn't come fast enough. When payday finally rolled around, he sent most of his monthly $250 stipend to his mom. With the few bucks he held on to, he treated himself to a real nice outfit — and some new underwear, too. He pitched the old stuff into the trash and never looked back. From that point on, it was his goal to only cover himself in nice clothes.

It did not take long for Satchel to become an absolute star. Natural talent and hard work made him an incredible athlete, and his pitching ability exploded with the experience he was gathering on the mound. Fans watched him pitch shutouts and no-hitters and were delighted by the drama of dust-ups and confrontations with players and umps he always seemed to find his way into. Satchel put on a show wherever he went, and the crowds started coming to witness not just his pitching, but his enormous personality. Ticket sales skyrocketed.

To the frustration of many team owners, Satchel didn't pay much attention to the contracts that he signed. Any given year he might pitch for four or five different teams, bouncing around from town to town. Wherever they were paying, he'd happily show up to pitch. Despite this nomadic approach to teams, he earned a spot on the biggest field of his career up to that point. A series of exhibition games between Negro League All-Stars and all-white Major League All-Stars would give him the chance to prove himself against the players everyone knew from the papers and the radio. Just like he knew he would, Satchel stood out and gave the white players fits. Legendary New York Yankee Joe DiMaggio said Paige was the best pitcher he'd ever seen.

Satchel could whip a baseball by just about anyone and leave them dumbfounded. It didn't matter what they looked like, where they came from, or what they believed. Satchel struck them all out. There was even a famous barnstorming team filled with fanatically religious men who believed it was a sin to cut their beards and hair. In addition to the hair thing, these guys believed the world would be ending soon. Might as well go out having fun, they must've thought. Playing baseball with beards down to their belts was a way to pass the time and save some souls. Satchel struck them out, too. They  must've been impressed, because afterwards they actually hired him to pitch a few games for their team. Satchel never gave a clear answer on whether or not he wore a fake beard to fit in.

It is believed that at the height of his career in the Negro Leagues he was earning more money than the president of the United States, and certainly more than most of the players in the Major Leagues. He had a chauffeur to drive his big fancy car around. Stuffed into his beautiful luggage cases, he had 40 of the finest suits, all tailored to his long, lanky frame. Gone were the days of rough sackcloth undies, or (if he was lucky) some cotton hand-me downs. Satchel filled his closets and suitcases with custom-made underwear of every color, sporting vivid flower patterns and made of the softest silk money could buy.

Despite all the silk and flowers, one big thorn stuck in his side. He couldn't play in the Majors. The attention and fame he earned had done a lot to fight racism simply by proving that an African-American man could play, earn, and entertain as well as (or better than, if we're being honest) any white athletes.

But it was not Satchel who would break the color barrier in baseball in 1947. It was his former teammate, a 28-year-old phenom named Jackie Robinson. The next year, the Cleveland Indians, hot in pursuit of a World Series championship, called on Satchel Paige to join the Major League team. When he made his debut, he was 42 years old — by far the oldest "rookie" in baseball.

Cleveland would win the World Series that year, with a lot of help from Satchel, but the rest of his six years in the Majors would not be as impressive as his career in other leagues. By the time he left the Majors he was almost 50. You can do a lot when you're 50, but dominating professional baseball is not usually one of those things.

Even though he was retired, his legend grew, and there were not many names that excited baseball fans like Satchel's. So in 1965, when the owner of the Kansas City Athletics wanted to bring out a huge crowd, he knew just what to do. He created "Satchel Paige Appreciation Night" and hired the 59-year-old hurler to take to the mound and prove that he still had plenty of gas in the tank.

Satchel didn't shy away from the chance to put on a show. The audience roared with laughter as he sat next to the bullpen, gently rocking in a rocking chair, looking like an old man. Occasionally a nurse would come by to check on him. It was all an act, like the pre-show drama in professional wrestling. When they called him to the mound, he moved like a man half his age.

This was the moment he became the oldest man to play professional baseball. While some people doubted his physical ability at this age, Satchel had nothing but confidence in himself. He pitched for three innings and gave up only one hit — every other batter was sent back to the dugout in shame.

After throwing his last pitch, a pitch that would be the last of his remarkable career, he stood on the diamond and soaked in the adoration of a well-deserved standing ovation. Before the fans had a chance to finish, he tipped his cap one last time, smiled, and headed to the locker room to clean up. He had already taken off his pants when someone rushed in to the locker room looking for the pitcher. The messenger found Satchel standing there in nothing but his underwear. Satchel was surprised to hear they wanted him back on the field. This was confusing, because once a player leaves the game, he can't go back in. Satchel pulled his pants back up over his underwear and as he made it to the door he heard a stadium full of people  singing. Standing on the field again, he realized the song was for him. The crowd, now holding candles and lighters up, cheered when he reappeared, and sang a song, "Old Gray Mare," for the one and only Satchel Paige.

It was a good thing he put his pants back on.

BABE RUTH,
ALL-STAR UNDERWEAR ADVERTISER

Professional athletes endorsing products like deodorant, cars, and t-shirts isn't anything new. In the 1920s, baseball star Babe Ruth was the king of selling stuff. The celebrity slugger had more endorsement contracts than any other sports star before him. When not hitting home runs (which he did a lot) or striking out (which he also did a lot), The Great Bambino used his image to sell sodas, gum, and even underwear. The union suit bearing his name and face on the front of the box came with the testimonial, "It's never ripped out the back, like some underwear I've seen." In 1927, one pair of "Babe Ruth All America Athletic Underwear" cost fans one dollar.

Australian Gold Medal Gag

Since the 1930s, the Olympics opening ceremony has included a torch relay, which attracts onlookers eager to glimpse the Olympic flame as it makes its way to light the symbolic cauldron to officially start the games. In 1956, one cheeky college student pranked a crowd full of Australian Olympics enthusiasts and even the Lord Mayor of Sydney, with little more than a table leg and a pair of underwear.

Barry Larkin did not like the fact that the torch relay tradition had actually been founded during the 1936 Olympics in Berlin, Germany, which was organized by Hitler's Nazi Party. To show his disdain, he made a torch of his own. He spray-painted a table leg silver and put a tin can on top. Into the cup he placed kerosene-soaked underwear. When he came running along the route with the undies ablaze, everyone assumed that he was the official torch bearer rather than a college student pulling their legs. He handed the brief-burning beacon to the clueless mayor, who began his speech while the smoke of flaming undies filled his nostrils. Everyone was surprised when the real torch showed up. By that time, Larkin was long gone.

Unfrozen Underwear Model
Otzi The Iceman (sometime during the Ice Age)

Underwear is kinda funny. In many cases, we don't know much about what people wear underneath because most prefer to only share their clothes on the outside. Despite the fact that we probably all have underwear on right now, it's still easy to get uptight and tight-lipped about our tightey-whities.

Most people from the past felt the same way, if not more so. In other cases — say, prehistoric times — there's no way to know what people wore, simply because very little has survived.

This makes for an exciting discovery when someone like Otzi shows up . But let his story serve as a warning to you: If you are unfortunate enough to be frozen in ice, please make sure you have on clean underwear. Otzi's mother might have been embarrassed to learn about the look of his undies when he made his surprise appearance. To put it bluntly, his undies might have been tight, but they were definitely not very white.

As you probably know, countries fight about a lot of things. Usually they fight about big things, but international conflicts have also been sparked by such seemingly small stuff as pigs rooting in the wrong place, a runaway dog, and even one measly ear that used to be attached to the head of some guy named Jenkins[7]. Only once in history have two nations fought over a dead guy in his dirty underwear. Luckily, the would-be "War for Otzi and his Undies" never got violent and was resolved relatively quickly. Inspired by Otzi's chill demeanor (and chillier body temperature), cooler heads prevailed. Militaries never even got involved. Instead, Italy and Austria turned to the real authorities: scientists.

Austria and Italy are very close. In fact, they share a border. This border (or the disagreement about where it begins and ends) was precisely the problem. No one really cares about a boundary line until something valuable is on that boundary, and in 1991, one of the most valuable discoveries of all time was made along this particular

---

[7] The War of Jenkins's Ear was a war between England and Spain that went on for nine years. Seems excessive for an ear, right?

border. It wasn't buried treasure or jewels — it was a dead body. But because this dead body was found high up in the rocky and jagged 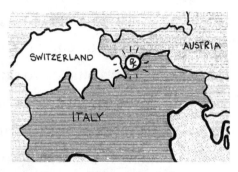 Alpine Mountains, it was tricky to determine the *exact* location of this boundary.

The drama began with an unsuspecting couple heading out for a hike while on vacation. The German visitors were near the Otztal Valley region of the Alps, where the powder-white snowcaps and craggy cliffs are as picturesque as a gift shop postcard. Clearly, these travelers were not the kind of people to sit around and enjoy the stunning scenery from a distance. They came to experience the majesty of the mountains up close and personal.

If you're the type who likes cold, strenuous activity, a day like this is probably as fun as it gets. At least until you come upon a dead body, which is *exactly* how this vacation got ruined. Lucky for them, the couple was clad in clean underwear (at least until they were surprised by a corpse). The same could not be said for the man in their path. They stopped dead in their tracks at the sight. Dark and twisted, the lower part of the lifeless body seemed to be frozen into the icy mountainside — right around the top of his raggedy brown underwear.

Wishing to help and hoping for the best, the hikers initially sprang into action but quickly concluded there was nothing they could do to save the iceman. One close look and they knew that no amount of mouth-to-mouth resuscitation or CPR would bring him back to life.

They knew it was wrong to just leave him, though. Perhaps there had been a crime, they thought. Or at the very least, what if this poor dead guy was a fellow hiker who had overdone it, disappeared, and died while someone somewhere was missing him ?

They immediately headed to a station on the trail and alerted authorities, but when the Alpine emergency workers rushed to the scene, they found a job out of their league. This was not the sort of rescue they were qualified to do. Instead, they called in the real authorities: scientists.

Before the scientists could arrive to secure the scene, the people present tried to pry the body from the permafrost. The torso, head, and arms were mostly out of the ice, but from the waist down, the cold, crusty fellow was firmly stuck, like a greedy arm caught in a vending machine. Little progress was made, so they crowdsourced the labor: anyone who happened by on the trail was invited to take a few whacks at the earth surrounding the iceman.

Word to the wise: don't let random people do delicate work. While they thought they were being helpful, this recklessness left the specimen with some serious damage. When the scientists finally figured out what they were dealing with, the thought of these random passersby poking and prodding at the iceman was petrifying. This wasn't a freshly dead body. It wasn't even a pretty old body. After running radiocarbon tests, scientists discovered the man had  been dead for over *5,000 years!* Imagine the relief the hikers felt that they hadn't tried to give him mouth-to-mouth resuscitation.

Frozen or not, everyone needs a name. Because of his location in the Otztal Valley, the scientists naturally started calling him Otzi. The discovery was incredible. Old bodies had been found before, but nothing in his condition. While Otzi's head, shoulders, knees, and toes[8] were certainly exciting, some people were even more excited by what was found with him: all of his stuff. Originally, it was the assumption that the dirty brown loin-

---

[8] …and partially eaten butt. Seems some ancient animal might've made a meal of his buns, way back when.

cloth around his waist was all he carried from his previous life. The melting ice around him revealed much more.

Across the sea in Egypt, a myriad of mummies had been recovered with plenty of physical possessions. The problem is that none of these are very realistic collections of the things a person might have actually used in their day-to-day life. The perished pharaohs and mortal mummies were buried with all of the stuff that their friends thought they might need for a splendid afterlife — fancy dishes, vats of honey, fine clothes, and of course plenty of changes of underwear. Had any normal person just died alone, on a random day in a random place, like poor Otzi, the things they carried and wore would have been very different. Obviously, plenty of people have died this way, but if they're still out there, we haven't found them yet.

Lucky for us, some 5,000 years ago, before Otzi's body could moulder or be eaten by wild animals, he was covered in a snowfall, frozen, and eventually gobbled up by the ice of a glacier. For centuries, Otzi would remain completely unseen by the world around him until he slowly melted out to surprise a pair of poor vacationers. Not wanting to embarrass the iceman, doctors covered his nearly naked body and carried him down the mountain to a nearby super-sized refrigerator in Austria. Even a centuries-old body immediately begins to decompose if it warms up, so it was important to keep him on ice, like a tub of Grandma's egg salad.

While the temperature in the refrigerator dropped, the dispute outside over who should keep the dead guy heated up. The hikers had discovered him right on the border of Italy and Austria, with the Italians claiming that he was found on their side of the imaginary line. He was rightfully theirs, they believed. But Otzi was already comfortably nestled in Austria, and the Austrians respectfully disagreed with Italy about the boundary line. They planned on keeping Otzi cold in their walk-in freezer for the rest of his days. The disagreement got pretty serious. Who knew a dead guy in his underwear could be such a commodity?

International law doesn't settle matters by having presidents play "Rock, Paper, Scissors" for cold corpses. Instead, they got their final answer from those authoritative scientists. After some precise GPS measurements were taken of Otzi's final resting place, it was confirmed that the Italians were correct — the dead guy in underwear was their dead guy in underwear. An odd victory celebration followed and then they began making plans for the cold old man. Not only would it be amazing to learn about life in the past from him, but they also realized tourists would travel from far and wide to see poor Otzi in his underwear.

There were still hurdles to clear, though. Threats were made from would-be mummy-nappers in Austria who shivered at the idea of the Austrian Iceman becoming the oldest and coldest Italian citizen. It was serious. Officials believed some- one would try to steal the crusty old thing, so they  spared nothing when it came to precautions. The super- dead, nearly naked man was — no joke — loaded into an ambulance (several years too late, mind you) and given a multi-car police escort over the border to Italy.

With the body snatchers subdued, Otzi was nestled into his new safe house. Still today, he rests on the same glass slab in a moisture- and temperature-controlled room in Bolzano, Italy. If the poor guy could've spoken, he probably would've said he just wanted some peace and quiet. But you know how scientists are. Sure, they're experts about a lot of stuff, but when it comes to poking and prodding at an old specimen such as Otzi, they just can't help themselves.

HALL OF FAME

HAIR SHIRT

In the early days of Christianity, some people showed their religious commitment in some pretty extreme ways. Kneeling for hours, walking for months on a pilgrimage, or fasting (which means not eating), were several ways people paid penance in the Middle Ages. Another way, which still survives today, is going to confession. At the time, if someone admitted their sins and wished to atone, they might have found themselves wearing a hair shirt. The unluckiest might have also found hair pants under their clothes, too.

These shirts and underpants were made from coarsely woven animal hair (usually goat) which was super-duper uncomfortable against naked skin. That was the idea.

Many believed that the discomfort was a necessary reminder to always be on one's best behavior.

Many rich and powerful people wore these itchy goat hair underwear as reminder to stay humble despite their earthly accomplishments. It is said that King Charlemagne, one of the most powerful kings in history, was buried wearing a hair shirt underneath his fine linens — just in case he forgot to be humble in the afterlife.

Years later, people saw these hair shirts as a way to get a confession out of prisoners. Guilty or not, people would often confess just to take the itchy underwear off.

Worn Out

Meriwether Lewis (1774–1809)
William Clark (1770–1838)

The Lewis and Clark Expedition might sound a lot like the scenic road trips many people take today. There were strenuous hikes, nights camping under the stars, dinners cooked over an open flame, thousands of itchy mosquito bites, and very few opportunities to take a bath — all of which might sound familiar to anyone who's taken a family camping trip.

Since it took place in the early 1800s, their road trip didn't include a road, a car, or a single cheesy roadside attraction along the way. An occasional souvenir shop would have come in handy because, despite being ready to head deep into the wilderness for years, these grown men were not ready to give up the thrill of opening presents. Holidays on the road would still be days to share gifts. Unfortunately their gift options were constantly dwindling.

Meriwether Lewis and William Clark were the men who organized the trek, and the group of 30 or so road trippers they put together became known as the Corps of Discovery. The Corps left St. Louis, Missouri, in 1804 on a two-year journey across the American continent. The main goal of the expedition was to find a water route across the North American Continent to the Pacific Ocean. They failed. Mostly because no such thing exists. It quickly became clear that the Rocky Mountains are a pretty big obstacle for anyone trying to take a boat from the Mississippi River to the Pacific Ocean.

Luckily, coast-to-coast boat traffic wasn't their only goal. They were more successful with other matters, including the hundreds of plants and animals they'd see that were unfamiliar to non-Native people. The American government asked Lewis and Clark to collect specimens, draw, and describe as many of these as they could in excruciating detail. They filled volumes with pictures of birds, bears, and bitterroot flowers. Additionally, they were also asked to establish trade relationships with the Native Americans on whose land they were encroaching. About a year into to the trip they famously met a Shoshone woman named Sacagawea.

Simply preparing for the nearly never-ending camping trip was a job most people would struggle with. Since there was no way of knowing how long the trip was going to take, they had to find the balance between what they could carry, and what they would need most. Lewis and Clark gathered a group of backwoods men who felt at home in the forests, who could read maps and hunt bears, and who were okay with wearing the same clothes for days on end. Packing enough stuff for the whole trip was impossible, and the men of the Corps knew it, but they brought heaps of food, clothing, tools, trade goods, gunpowder, and even a few Christmas gifts.

One helpful thing about the Corps of Discovery is that they kept very detailed journals, so it's easy to go back and learn all kinds of things about their adventure. Their first Christmas was uneventful, perhaps because it happened before the journey really got underway. In his journal entry for the holiday, William Clark just wrote that the men "frolicked and hunted all day." Gifts weren't mentioned in detail, but since they were still so early into the adventure, it's believed that they had plenty of stuff to make their holiday celebration festive.

That spring, when it was warm enough to finally start the 2300-mile trek to the Pacific Ocean, the men made sure to dress their best. Along with several others, co-captains Lewis and Clark had full woolen military uniforms.

In hindsight, they would probably agree that they were a tad overdressed. If you know anything about wool, you know that it's less than ideal for hot summer days.

The men had underwear in between their sensitive skin and that scratchy, stinky, sweat-seizing wool, but this flannel underwear didn't look like the white cotton underwear you might unwrap at a gift exchange and then disappointedly toss aside to wait patiently for something more fun. This underwear was more like a long shirt with billowy sleeves. No boxers. No briefs. Nothing with a waistband of any kind, in fact. The explorers would take the long front and long back of the shirt and tuck them between their legs in the place of underpants.

As they made their way across the continent in their diaper-shirts, the clothes on their backs quickly wore out, tore to tatters, or just became generally uncomfortable. The men were rugged. Their clothes were not. Out in the west, they were several decades away from the existence of a department store, so they had to improvise and adapt. When those clothes wore out, they started making pants, shoes, and overshirts from the hides of the animals they ate. And they ate a lot of animals. While working their way through the Great Plains, the men typically stuffed about nine pounds of meat into their hungry mouths each day. Lucky for them there was a lot of game to hunt in the Great Plains, because these bowling-ball-sized portions of meat were pretty necessary.

The big boat they brought along did a good job of holding supplies, but not a very good job moving on its own. Fighting against the current of Missouri River was tough, and since it was rare that there was enough wind to fill the sails, another energy source was needed. Some men spent their time hunting the Great Plains to supply the expedition's men with their daily ration of buffalo humps and beaver tails. Most of them, however, found themselves working up a nine-pound hunger by wading through the muddy shore with wet undies as they pulled the giant boat upriver.

Since the Missouri River is the longest river in North America, this was a tall order. Imagine the relief the boat-haulers must've felt when they finally stopped for a winter break with the Mandan 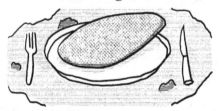 people, in the area that is now North Dakota. After building a fort on the riverbank, which they named Fort Mandan, they set about to trade with the Mandan villagers, stay warm, and plan for the next leg of the journey.

It was here that they met a French trapper named Charbonneau, who had been living in the Native American village on the other side of the river with his young, pregnant wife, Sacagawea[9]. Knowing the journey was far from over, Lewis and Clark agreed that they could use some help for the mysteries ahead of them. Charbonneau, his not-really-wife Sacagawea, and her soon-to-be-born baby were enlisted to join them just as soon as the river unfroze.

The winter of 1804 was colder than a polar bear's toenail. It's tough to party under frigid circumstances, but they refused to let sub-zero temperatures put a damper on the Christmas celebrations. Construction on their winter fort finished on December 23rd, giving them just enough time to cut loose. On Christmas Eve, possibly hinting at a hankering for some spicy pies, Lewis and Clark bestowed upon each of the men the curious gifts of flour, dried apples, and pepper. Kinda makes unwrapping a new pack of underwear sound pretty good, doesn't it?

Undeterred by the lack of exciting presents, the men woke William Clark on Christmas morning with the celebratory firing of rifles. Never one to break up a good

---

[9] Listen, to call her his "wife" is pretty unfair. She was only like 14, and was actually purchased from a rival tribe as a slave, of sorts. It's kinda gross and sad, but that doesn't take anything away from the fact that Sacagawea was 100% awesome. There were many times she proved her bravery and skill — actually, way more than Charbonneau did. He was sort of a coward.

party, Clark gave the group permission to fire a cannon on the boat three times in celebration. When it came to getting their holly-jollies on the frontier, they took what they could get. For the remainder of the holiday, the men hunted and danced (but probably not at the same time). By nine o'clock everyone was happy, tired, and possibly full of spicy pie.

Once the spring thaw finally came, the expedition continued west along the Missouri River. Along for the trek were not only Sacagawea, but also her baby, who earned the nickname Pompey. Despite a lack of diapers on the frontier, the happy baby was a welcome part of the team, but he would have to be carried most of the time. Because the big boat wouldn't make it far up the narrowing waters, the members decided to set out on foot to the Rocky Mountains. It was bound to be a brutal hike, but luckily, their new companion Sacagawea helped them get some horses from the Shoshone people. Now they could tick horseback riding off their road trip adventure checklist.

The Rocky Mountains were no easy trek, though, and after going without food for days, some of the men began to wonder how those poor horses might

taste. With only the occasional berry bush to offer nourishment, they were far from the daily nine-pound meat meals the Great Plains had provided. In the nick of time, the starving party arrived at a village of Nez Perce people. The Nez Perce nursed them back to health and offered plenty of alternatives to horse meat. Some were more appetizing than others.

One food, known as Chinook Olives to the men, began as acorns. On their own, plain acorns are not easily digested by humans. To make them edible, acorns were collected in a pit dug in the soil. For weeks, men of the village visited the pit when they  needed to relieve themselves. The pee-pickling process left the nut inside edible and nourishing. Before being munched, the acorns were roasted in the coals of a hot fire. This took care of the urine stench and reportedly left them not just edible, but quite tasty. (Maybe don't try this at home).

Once they had their strength back, the Corps of Discovery again began to think about getting to the Pacific Ocean, which was now closer than ever. The Columbia River would be a sure-fire path to the coast, but canoes would be a better vehicle than their not-so-delicious horses. If they were fortunate enough to return, they'd need those horses again, though. In an act of friendship, the Nez Perce offered to horse-sit while they canoed to the coast over the months ahead. Clearly, any gifts the men received on the journey would pale in comparison to the gifts of the Nez Perce.

By the time they were finally staring at the Pacific Ocean, the seasons were changing again. A vote was held on whether to stay for winter, or hurry back to the horses. Knowing the return journey could be much faster, especially during the warm seasons, the group thought one last winter fort would be the safest choice. One last winter fort meant the men would spend one final Christmas together.

Unhampered by the constant fog and damp cold of the Pacific Coast winter, the party started early again. Despite the short supply of gunpowder now, Clark awoke on Christmas morning again to the sound of celebratory rifle shots. Nearly all of their supplies had been used up, lost in capsized canoes, or traded to the many Native Americans they had met over the last two years. Even their feast that day was described by William Clark as "A bad Christmass diner."

"Our Diner concisted of pore Elk, So much Spoiled that we eate it thro' mear necessity. Some Spoiled pounded fish and a fiew roots," he wrote.

Clark never really learned how to spell very well, but despite that, the rest of the group really liked him and joined him in a one-star meal of spoiled elk, fish, and some not-so delicious roots. They also got creative when it came to that year's Christmas gifts. Sacagawea surprised him with two dozen weasel tails, and another member of the Corps got crafty and made Clark a brand new pair of leather moccasins.

As if weasel tails and moccasins for the long hike home weren't enough,  Clark also received a peculiar gift from his friend and co-captain, Meriwether Lewis. In his usual poor spelling, Clark wrote, "I recved a presnt of Capt L. of a fleece hosrie Shirt Draws and Socks."

Socks are socks, as you certainly know. As for the "hosrie shirt" and "Draws" he mentions, well, he's mentioning unmentionables. At this point in the drawn-out journey, William Clark was surely surprised to get underwear for Christmas.

The looming question is, where did this underwear come from? They were deep into their journey and by necessity these guys were using everything they had. The most logical explanation is that his pal Lewis gave him a set of underwear he had already worn. Considering how hard things were to come by on the trail, he had probably worn them a lot, actually. The gift from Lewis to Clark was very thoughtful, and much appreciated, even if it was a rank re-gift of butt-rubbing regalia.

Clark couldn't waste them, though, and he probably got plenty of use from the undies on the long (but much quicker) journey back home. Things move much faster when you're riding a river's current. When the continental travelers finally arrived back at St. Louis in 1806, one of the first things they did was buy some new clothes. Certainly, clean, unworn undies were on the shopping list.

New Year, New Underwear

New Year's Eve is a time for good-luck traditions all over the world. Toting a packed suitcase for a quick walk around the block is a way some people guarantee an adventurous new year. Others sweep dirt from their homes out the front door, gobble grapes at midnight, or eat cabbage and corned beef the next morning to bring good fortune.

In some South American countries like Brazil, the color of underwear you wear when the clock strikes midnight can impact the year ahead. Colors have different meanings, but yellow is considered the luckiest color to have underneath your clothes. No guarantees, but it's worth a shot!

Alan Greenspan's Underwear Index

Economists are always looking for clues on how people feel about spending money. One famous economist used underwear to figure it out. Alan Greenspan served five terms as the chair of America's Federal Reserve and he popularized a measurement known as the Men's Underwear Index. The idea is simple. You can see how strong the national economy is based on how many pairs of men's underwear are being purchased. When money is tight, an average man will stretch the life of his tighteywhities. If things are financially sound, then men are more willing to toss out the worn-outs, and treat themselves to some fancy underpants. Fresh undies indicate a booming economy.

Acknowledgments

There are a lot of people to thank for the support I've had along the way. I'm grateful to so many, but especially to my wife, Sarah.

Others I wish to thank:
Lisa, Mom, and Jim, and my late father Barry Sullivan, whose life I strive to honor every day.

The Sullivan family — especially my grandfather Jack Sullivan, who taught me to appreciate the past and look for connections.

The Noe family — especially my cousin Keith Guetig for all the encouragement, but also for teaching me about the power of a funny song at a young age.

The Buccolas

Rachel Platt, Megan Schanie, Brian West, Heather Gotlib, Tony Dingman, Eric Frantz, Kelly Moore, Ve Reibel, Andy Treinen, AJ Cornell, Melinda Beck, Jodi Lewis (who gave me my first real shot at this kind of work), and everyone else in my Frazier Museum family, past and present.

Stephen Kertis and Ben Kemble for taking a shot on my first book, *The Meatshower*. And especially to Shae Goodlett for being gung-ho to illustrate something so strange.

Amber Thieneman, Rob Collier, Jason Lawrence, Brigid Kaelin, Chris Rodahaffer, Dave Howard, Scott Moore, and my Squeezebot pals.

Jon Heck, Robert Woodford, Andrew Winkler, Ryan Potter, Ike Phillips, Joe Burchett, Dan Henderson, and the Starduck Charities crew.

The entire Kids Listen family, including Eric O'Keefe, Polly Hall, Pamela Rogers, Lynn Hickernell, Melly Victor, Dan Saks, Lindsay Patterson, and Ali Wilkinson.

Jennie Cole

My dear friend Suki Anderson, of course.

Lori — what a stroke of luck our meeting was. And Lisa. Thanks to both of you for believing in this.

Thanks to all the Patreon and Kickstarter people and every single person who has listened to *The Past and The Curious*. You have made this journey so much fun!

I believe the world is a better place because these people are in it. I'm just grateful that we are connected. Good people make the world go 'round. I know you'll continue to find them in your life, too. Good people are everywhere.

BIBLIOGRAPHY

Selected Bibliography

Chapter 1: I See Lincoln's Underpants — Abraham Lincoln

Goodwin, Doris Kearns. *Team of Rivals: The Political Genius of Abraham Lincoln.* London: Penguin, 2013.

Gorsline, Douglas. "The Clothes Lincoln Wore," *American Heritage* magazine, Volume 8, Issue 5, August 1957.

Guelzo, Allen. *Lincoln and Douglas: The Debates That Defined America.* New York: Simon & Schuster, 2014.

Lamb, Brian, Susan Swain, and Patrick G. Lawlor. *Abraham Lincoln: Great American Historians on Our Sixteenth President.* New York: Perseus Books Group, 2009.

McCullough, David. *The Great Bridge: The Epic Story of the Building of the Brooklyn Bridge.* New York: Simon & Schuster, 1972.

Widmer, Edward L., Clay Risen, and George Kalogerakis. *The New York Times: Disunion: 106 Articles from the New York Times Opinionator.* New York: Black Dog & Leventhal Publishing, 2013.

Chapter 2: No Privacy For The Queen — Marie Antoinette

Baker, Keith Michael. *What Life Was Like During the Age of Reason: France, AD 1660–1800.* New York: Time-Life Education, 1999.

Fraser, Antonia. *Marie Antoinette.* Paris: Flammarion, 2009.

Marie Antoinette and the French Revolution. Written and Directed by David Grubin, David Grubin Productions, Inc. 2006. https://www.pbs.org/marieantoinette/.

Weber, Caroline. *Queen of Fashion: What Marie Antoinette Wore To The Revolution.* London: Aurum, 2008.

Chapter 3: Caught With His Pants Down — Charles Lee vs. George Washington

Chernow, Ron. *Washington: A Life.* London: Allen Lane, 2010.

Lee, Charles. "Charles Lee to Benjamin Rush." *The Pennsylvania Magazine of History and Biography* 67, no. 3 (1943): 286–89. http://www.jstor.org/stable/20087603.

Mazzagetti, Dominick. *Charles Lee: Self Before Country.* New Brunswick: Rutgers University Press, 2013.

McCullough, David. *1776.* New York: Simon & Schuster, 2005.

Papas, Phillip. *Renegade Revolutionary: The Life of General Charles Lee.* New York: New York University Press, 2014.

Chapter 4: Underdressed Rescue — Garrett Morgan

DiCicco, Joan. *The Unstoppable Garrett Morgan: Inventor, Entrepreneur, Hero.* New York: Lee & Low Books, 2019.

Gates, Henry Louis, Evelyn Brooks Higginbotham. *African American Lives.* Oxford University Press, 2004.

King, William M. "Guardian of the Public Safety: Garrett A. Morgan and the Lake Erie Crib Disaster." *The Journal of Negro History* 70, no. 1/2 (1985): 1–13. http://www.jstor.org/stable/2717634.

Morgan, Garrett A. *The Encyclopedia of Cleveland.* A joint effort by Case Western University and the Western Reserve Historical Society. February 23, 2005. Retrieved January 20, 2022.

Chapter 5: Up, Up, And Away Went Their Clothes — John Jeffries and Jean-Pierre Blanchard

Darling, David. *The Rocket Man and Other Extraordinary Characters in the History of Flight.* London: Oneworld Publications, 2013.

Holmes, Richard. *Falling Upwards: How We Took to the Air.* London: Harper-Collins Publishers, 2013.

Jeffries, John. *A Narrative of the Two Aerial Voyages of Doctor Jeffries with Mons. Blanchard.* London: J. Robson, New Bond-Street, 1786.

Olshan, Matthew. *A Voyage in the Clouds: The (Mostly) True Story of the First International Flight by Balloon in 1785.* New York: Farrar, Straus, Giroux, 2016.

Wright, Sharon. *Balloonomania Belles.* Barnsley: Pen & Sword History, 2018.

Chapter 6: Stuck in a Stinky Trunk — *Mona Lisa*

Hoobler, Dorothy, and Thomas Hoobler. *The Crimes of Paris.* New York: Little, Brown, 2009.

Isaacson, Walter. *Leonardo da Vinci.* New York: Simon & Schuster, 2017.

Kemp, Martin. *Leonardo Da Vinci : The 100 Milestones.* New York: Sterling 2019.

"Theft of Mona Lisa: Topics in Chronicling America: Introduction." Theft of *Mona Lisa*, Library of Congress, https://guides.loc.gov/chronicling-america-theft-mona-lisa.

"Treasures of the World Home Page." PBS, Public Broadcasting Service, https://www.pbs.org/treasuresoftheworld/.

Chapter 7: Mermaid in Stockings — Annette Kellerman

Bohn, Michael. *Heroes & Ballyhoo: How the Golden Age of the 1920s Transformed American Sports.* Washington, DC: Potomac Books Inc., 2009.

Kellerman, Annette. *How to Swim.* New York: George H. Doran Company, 1918.

Taylor, Beth. "Annette Kellerman." National Film and Sound Archive of Australia, https://www.nfsa.gov.au/collection/curated/annette-kellerman. Accessed August 2020.

Walsh, G. P. *Australian Dictionary of Biography*. Melbourne University Press. 2010.

Wilk, Stephen R. *Lost Wonderland: The Brief and Brilliant Life of Boston's Million Dollar Amusement Park*. Amherst: Bright Leaf, an imprint of University of Massachusetts Press, 2020.

Chapter 8: Hanging By A Thread — John Wesley Powell

Dolnick, Edward. *Down the Great Unknown: John Wesley Powell's 1869 Journey of Discovery and Tragedy Through the Grand Canyon*. London: Harper Perennial, 2002.

Powell, J.W. *The Exploration of the Colorado River and Its Canyons*. New York: Dover Press (reprint), 1875.

Ross, John F. *The Promise of the Grand Canyon: John Wesley Powell's Perilous Journey and His Vision for the American West*. New York: Viking, 2018.

Worster, Donald. *A River Running West: The Life of John Wesley Powell*. New York: Oxford University Press, 2001.

Chapter 9: God Save The Queen's Undies — Queen Victoria

Baird, Julia. *Victoria the Queen: An Intimate Biography of the Woman Who Ruled an Empire*. New York: Random House, 2016.

Bondeson, Jan. *Queen Victoria's Stalker: The Strange Story of the Boy Jones*. Stroud, Gloucestershire: Amberley, 2012.

Wilson, A. N. *Victoria: A Life*, London: Atlantic Books, 2014.

Worsley, Lucy. *Queen Victoria — Daughter, Wife, Mother, Widow*. London: Hodder & Stoughton Ltd, 2018.

Chapter 10: Keep Your Friends Close, But Keep Your Underwear Closer — Al Capone

Eig, Jonathan. Get Capone: *The Secret Plot That Captured America's Most Wanted Gangster.* New York: Simon & Schuster, 2010.

Hoffman, Dennis E. *Scarface Al and the Crime Crusaders: Chicago's Private War Against Capone.* Carbondale: Southern Illinois University Press, 1993.

Kobler, John. *Capone: The Life and Times of Al Capone.* New York: Da Capo Press, 2003.

Chapter 11: Where No Man Has Gone Before — Buzz Aldrin

Aldrin, Buzz. *Magnificent Desolation: The Long Journey Home From the Moon.* New York: Three Rivers Press, 2010.

Cadbury, Deborah. *Space Race: The Epic Battle Between America and the Soviet Union for Dominance of Space.* New York: Harper Collins, 2006.

Chaikin, Andrew. *A Man on the Moon: The Voyages of the Apollo Astronauts.* London: Penguin Books, 2007.

Muir-Harmony, Teasel. *Apollo to the Moon.* Washington, DC: National Geographic, 2018.

Chapter 12: By The Seat Of His Pants — Buster Keaton

Dardis, Tom. *Keaton: The Man Who Wouldn't Lie Down.* New York: Limelight Editions, 1979.

Knopf, Robert. *The Theater and Cinema of Buster Keaton.* Princeton, NJ: Princeton University Press, 1999.

McPherson, Edward. *Buster Keaton: Tempest in a Flat Hat.* New York: Newmarket Press, 2005.

Meade, Marion. *Buster Keaton: Cut to the Chase.* New York City: HarperCollins, 1995.

Stevens, Dana. *Camera Man.* New York: Simon & Schuster, 2022.

Chapter 13: Eponymous Underpants — Amelia Bloomer

Bloomer, D. C. *Life and Writings of Amelia Bloomer.* Memphis: General Books, 2010.

Boissoneaul, Lorraine. "Amelia Bloomer Didn't Mean to Start a Fashion Revolution, But Her Name Became Synonymous With Trousers." *Smithsonian* magazine, May 24, 2018.

Buhle, Mari J., and Paul Buhle. *The Concise History of Woman Suffrage: Selections from the History of Woman Suffrage.* Urbana: University of Illinois Press, 2005. Print.

Songs of Women's Suffrage. Web. Retrieved from the Library of Congress, www.loc.gov/item/ihas.200197395/.

Strassel, Annemarie. "Designing Women: Feminist Methodologies in American Fashion." *Women's Studies Quarterly*, vol. 41, no. 1/2, 2012, pp. 35–59. JSTOR, http://www.jstor.org/stable/23611770. Accessed 5 Jan. 2020.

Chapter 14: From Burlap to Silk — Satchel Paige

Branson, Douglas M. *Greatness in the Shadows: Larry Doby and the Integration of the American League.* Lincoln, NE: London University of Nebraska Press, 2016.

Paige, Leroy (Satchel). *Maybe I'll Pitch Forever* (as told to David Lipman). University of Nebraska Press, 1993.

Tye, Larry. *Satchel: The Life and Times of an American Legend.* New York: Random House, 2009.

Tye, Larry. "Sizzling Satchel Paige." *American Heritage* magazine, Volume 60, Issue 1, Spring 2010. Accessed online July 15, 2019. https://www.americanheritage.com/sizzling-satchel-paige.

Chapter 15 Unfrozen Underwear Model — Otzi

Fowler, Brenda. *Iceman: Uncovering the Life and Times of a Prehistoric Man Found in an Alpine Glacier.* New York: Random House, 2000.

"Otzi the Iceman." Museo Archeologico Dell'Alto Adige, https://www.iceman.it/en/clothing/.

Spindler, Konrad. *The Man in the Ice: The Preserved Body of a Neolithic Man Reveals the Secrets of the Stone Age.* Translated by Ewald Osers. London: Phoenix, 2001.

Pinkowski, Jennifer. "Otzi the Iceman: What we know 30 years after his discovery." *National Geographic*, September 15, 2021. https://www.nationalgeographic.com/history/article/tzi-the-iceman-what-we-know-30-years-after-his-discovery

Chapter 16: Worn Out — Lewis and Clark

Ambrose, Stephen E. *Undaunted Courage: Meriwether Lewis, Thomas Jefferson, and the Opening of the American West.* Simon and Schuster, New York, 1996.

Bergon, Frank, editor. *The Journals of Lewis and Clark.* Penguin Classics, New York, 1989.

Gilman, Carolyn. *Lewis and Clark: Across the Divide.* Washington, DC: Smithsonian Books, 2003.

Tubbs, Stephenie A., and Clay S. Jenkinson. *The Lewis and Clark Companion: An Encyclopedic Guide to the Voyage of Discovery.* New York: H. Holt, 2003.

General Sources:

Cunnington, C. Willett, and Phillis Cunnington. *The History of Underclothes.* New York: Dover Publications, 1992.

Fischer, David Hackett. *Albion's Seed.* New York: Oxford University Press, 1989.

Fleming, Candace. *Ben Franklin's Almanac: Being a True Account of the Good Gentleman's Life.* New York: Atheneum Books for Young Readers, 2003.

Griffin, Gary. *The History of Men's Underwear.* Los Angeles: Added Dimension Publishing, 1991.

Gunn, Tim, and Ada Calhoun. *Tim Gunn's Fashion Bible.* New York: Gallery Books, 2012.

Huey, Lois Miner. *Ick! Yuck! Eew! Our Gross American History*. Minneapolis: Milbrook Press, 2014.

Kelly, Ian. *Beau Brummell : The Ultimate Dandy*. London: Hodder and Stoughton, 2005.

Klara, Robert. *The Hidden White House: Harry Truman and the Reconstruction of America's Most Famous Residence*. New York: St. Martin's Press, 2014.

Larson, Erik. *Thunderstruck*. New York: Three Rivers Press, 2006.

Marzio, Peter, editor. *A Nation of Nations*. New York: Harper and Row, 1979.

Morley, Jacqueline. *Fashion: The History of Clothes: A Compact Guide: From Prehistory to the Designer Decades*. Brighton: Book House, 2015.

Reich, Howard, and William Gaines. *Jelly's Blues: The Life, Music, and Redemption of Jelly Roll Morton*. Cambridge: Da Capo, 2003.

Varga, Vincent. *Eyes of the Nation: A Visual History of the United States*. New York: Portland House, 1997.

About the Author

Mick Sullivan is the creator and producer of *The Past and The Curious: A History Podcast for Kids and Families*, a show which has been featured in *The New York Times, The Guardian, School Library Journal,* and more. He is the author of *The Meatshower: The Mostly True Tale of An Odd (and Somewhat Edible) Occurrence* and works at the Frazier History Museum in Louisville, KY. He lives with his wife and two sons, plays the banjo, and could probably use a nap.

About the Artist

Suki Anderson, whose constrictive underpants are affectionately nicknamed "Wonder Pants," is lucky to live just one block from Mick Sullivan in Louisville, KY. She helps tell stories in many ways, as an artist, designer, and singer. Her illustrated book *Dreams: Subconscious Fiction* was released for ludicrous dream lovers in 2019.